Glasgow
9 th

This b
be r
d

In Praise of Garrulous

By Allan Cameron

A polemic in which a garrulous and sceptical author
discourses at length on the wondrous nature of our
languages, our words, our uttered sounds or phonemes,
and pauses to consider the terrible destruction thereof
by dark and perhaps unconscious forces and foolishly
knowledgeable persons solely bent on the aggrandisement
of their power and the elimination of all that is diverse and
all the beauty of that diversity. An appeal to parliaments
everywhere and in particular to the one in the prosperous,
genteel and historic city of Edinburgh, capital of Scotland,
nation of talkative drunks and prim, pursed-lipped,
straight-backed and morally outraged savants, often the
same people at different times of day.

Vagabond Voices
Glasgow

© Allan Cameron 2008

First published in 2008 by Vagabond Voices

This edition published in 2013 by
Vagabond Voices Publishing Ltd.,
Glasgow,
Scotland.

ISBN 978-1-908251-24-4

The author's right to be identified as author of this book under
the Copyright, Designs and Patents Act 1988 has been asserted.

Printed and bound in Poland

Cover design by Mark Mechan

Typeset by Park Productions

For further information on Vagabond Voices, see the website,
www.vagabondvoices.co.uk

For Margaret

CONTENTS

Discourse cheers us to companionable reflection. Such reflection neither parades polemical opinion nor does it tolerate complaisant agreement. The sail of thinking keeps trimmed hard to the wind of the matter.
Martin Heidegger, *The Thinker as Poet*
(1947)

(The publisher added this quote as a kind of excuse: he feels that the author never was a good sailor and is likely to luff and to gybe, and then veer off in all directions)

Las lenguas, como las religiones, viven de herejías (Languages, like religions, thrive on heresies)
Miguel de Unamuno, "Contra el purismo", *Revista Nueva*, I, 8 (1899)

INTRODUCTION

Of what could all this lively world consist,
if not our well-intended intents to
fulfil ourselves in all we say and do.
Let these attempts to let my passions rip
fulfil ambitions of my clouded brain
which bring such sweetness to a life of pain
and plain monotone.

This is a book about language and above all about the value and essentiality of language in our lives. It might therefore be called a book on the "ecology" of language, because human language is in danger of being permanently damaged by the way modern technology has developed over the last century, and this will affect not only our competence in organising ourselves socially and politically, but also our inner selves. In other words, the process of homogenisation we call globalisation is not only damaging our external environment, but our internal one as well. At the same time, we are collectively accumulating an unprecedented mass of scientific and technological knowledge, which in a way we can be proud of, but only if individually and socially we retain our skills to deal with it. I believe the maintenance of our linguistic skills is essential to this task, and therefore the linguistic problem takes its place alongside all the other problems we face – problems with which any reasonably informed person is already fully acquainted.

Language is under attack on two fronts. Firstly, our language diversity is crumbling, and this is a problem that goes back perhaps even millennia, but the pace of language death is accelerating and is now no longer driven solely by imperial or bureaucratic realities. This particular aspect of the problem has been covered by many writers over the last decade or so. I was particularly impressed by David Crystal's *Language Death* (Cambridge: C.U.P., 2000) and Daniel Nettle's and Suzanne Romaine's *Vanishing Voices* (Oxford: O.U.P., 2000). Because this is a fairly well-trodden path, I have restricted myself to one fairly short chapter (Chapter Five), but nevertheless I think this is still the most important point in the language debate.

Secondly, our individual language skills are collapsing. This is partly the result of the previous point about the disappearance of language diversity, because monolingualism is not our natural state. This will seem counter-intuitive to many people living in Europe and particularly the Americas, because we have become so used over the last two hundred years to the idea of territorially homogeneous units called nation-states. Sub-Saharan Africa probably provides us with a better idea of a "natural" linguistic environment, in which people typically speak three or four "local languages" plus a lingua franca (often these languages have wonderfully intricate grammars and are occasionally very different from each other). Naturally such people are very accomplished linguistically, and it is not a strain for them because our brains are designed to cope (or rather the brains of young children are). But this is not the only force acting upon our linguistic skills, because early nationalism, the driving force behind linguistic homogenisation, was at least accompanied by a massive rise in literacy rates and assisted by the continuing presence of some linguistic diversity. The rise of cinema and television has displaced both reading (an artificial act well suited to our mental framework) and conversation (along with walking, the most natural of our activities for which we have been designed by evolution).

These core arguments run counter to most of the prevailing academic beliefs, and this book has to be placed within the context of that debate. To some extent, the question of the naturalness of language has been resolved by Chomsky, whose work constitutes a common departure point for moving in very different directions. A child is born with an instinct to learn language, or rather to learn languages. However, an ultra-Chomskyan line has been developed (Stephen Pinker), and its principal thesis is that all languages do the same things and are effectively interchangeable. A massive loss of our linguistic diversity might be a pity, but it will not affect us – the speakers of dominant languages. Fortunately other, mainly European, sociolinguists have carried out experiments that indicate that languages do indeed do things differently. Linguists call this argument the Sapir-Whorf thesis, and it was more popular before and just after the war. This is not some tiresome academic quibble, as it affects important matters of language policy and planning.

The naturalness of language and our potentially phenomenal linguistic skills mean that we ignore their cultivation at our peril. Just as our tendency always to take the car is affecting our physical health, so our tendency to remain confirmed monoglots, to read less and less, and to flop in front of the television instead of conversing between ourselves is damaging our intellectual and perhaps our mental health. I realise that this is entirely speculative at the moment and requires a more scientific approach from those who have the financial and academic resources to do so.[1]

---

1. It has to be said that many books of a general sociolinguistic nature remain anecdotal, while also asserting grand claims on the origins of language and the function of language without even entering into a reasoned analytical argument. I, at least, admit my shortcomings from the very beginning.

Who am I then to argue this case and with what authority do I speak? Well, first let me say that I wish to open or re-open a debate and not close it down. I have never written and I believe I never will write a book with such passion as this one. My passion on this subject has also made it a necessary book for me to write, but not an easy or perhaps even enjoyable one. It will always be my most autobiographical work, a kind of intellectual autobiography. My childhood homes were in Nigeria and what is now Bangladesh, but from the age of six I was sent to boarding schools. For our family holidays we sometimes went to the Highland village where my mother grew up. At the time Gaelic was losing ground, but still very much there. I was therefore at home in situations in which I could hear languages that I did not understand. And they fascinated me. Although proud of her Highland roots, my mother was not particularly interested in her linguistic ones. She came from a generation in which many people wished to divest themselves of a language they perceived as holding them back, and her parents tended to speak to her in English to help her "get on in life". Not everyone took this view: her cousin's family on the adjoining farm would only speak Gaelic in the home. But enough people were abandoning the language to make its future viability doubtful, and in fact mainland Gaelic was dying (although new urban pockets are now being created in Glasgow and Edinburgh, rather like "Dublin Irish"). In Bangladesh, I discovered I could learn Bengali and could sound reasonably convincing (in reality my pronunciation and sentence formation were better than my comprehension, and conversations tended to peter out because of this limitation; I did however take buses – take any bus going anywhere – just in order to meet up with Bengali-speakers who knew no English; I was showing the first symptoms of the obsessive language-learner). This discovery came as something of a surprise, as I was a complete failure at learning French in school, and sadly this inability or mental block has remained in spite of my enduring Francophilia. This, I believe, was partly due to the teachers I encountered and partly to the fact that some people retain a child's ability to learn languages for a bit longer – something that has nothing to do with the classroom situation. I joke that I have not learned more languages than anyone else, and I have certainly tinkered with several, while often being most interested in just seeing how they work.

This might not look a very distinguished linguistic background for anyone who wishes to speak authoritatively about language, but I did achieve one success: at the age of nineteen, I gave up my job working off-shore in the North Sea and bought a one-way ticket to Florence. I was thinking of travelling around Italy for six months and then returning to my former job. Instead I remained in Florence and put down roots perhaps deeper than I have ever put down elsewhere. It wasn't the sun, the wine, the food, the architecture or the art that I loved about Italy – although I much appreciated all those things – it was the language, particularly the language as I heard it in the streets with its Florentine directness and vulgar wit. This opened the way to Italian literature, which gave me another life (because I had already been an extremely well-read teenager). And most importantly for this justificatory passage, it led to my present situation: for the last fifteen years I have been translating books from Italian to English, and every day experiencing the problems of transferring one way of thinking into another. No book translator needs convincing that languages affect the way we interpret the world; he or she will struggle incessantly with the problems this undoubted fact creates for the profession, and fail, because translation can never produce an exact copy.

Although I believe that translation qualifies me more than

any other factor to write this book, I do not discuss it within these pages. Perhaps it is simply that I want to escape from work – from an activity in which I make judgements principally on the basis of long experience and therefore in a sense instinctively. However, the fact that the translation debate has been done to death by highly competent classical, Renaissance and modern writers means that I have little to add other than the anecdotal, which can be excessively dull for those not of the profession. In fact, I have attempted to keep all specific linguistic examples to an absolute minimum in order to make this book accessible to the non-specialist.

The only other language in which I have had a certain success, albeit a lesser one, is Gaelic, my mother's native tongue. But I did not learn it as part of some ethnic homecoming (when I was living in London in my twenties, I learned passable Welsh); I learned it because I was living in Glasgow for a few years and had always had an interest in minority languages. Gaelic is like Latin's cousin or second cousin perhaps. A case-based language with a vocative and no single word for "yes" and "no", it is a more ancient language than Welsh and the rest of the Brythonic group. Its elegant syntax makes it very different from other modern European languages (other than Irish, of course, which could be considered the same language). This experience has taught me something about the politics of minority languages.

I am very interested in how writing and printing have altered the way we speak and think, and this theme is an essential part of this book. I intentionally omit a detailed examination of how the internet, texting, e-mail and chat-rooms have affected language, although it would not surprise me if their influence turned out to be far-reaching. They are, in my opinion, the final stage in the centuries-long process whereby the written and spoken language have converged.

Text will become as instantaneous and unstructured as speech; it will lose those characteristics that have made it such a potent force in the development of our societies over the last five hundred years since the advent of printing. But of course, the structured written word will remain, possibly in the hands of an elite, and this is precisely the kind of development we must consciously attempt to avoid. On the whole, I have concentrated my arguments on the relative merits of telling stories in words or telling them in images. The latter being by far the most significant development and challenge to our linguistic competence.

Unsurprisingly I have found that this book is much better received by polyglots, while monoglot intellectuals, with some notable exceptions, resist it and perhaps take it as a blow to their *amour propre*. If they do, then they are very mistaken, because all arguments of this kind concern populations and not individuals. It is like the argument of the self-made man who in a society of huge inequalities uses his own case to claim there is equality of opportunity. The brilliance of some monoglot intellectuals is not in question: *In Praise of the Garrulous* is concerned with the general effects of expanding monolingualism and linguistic uniformity and conformity.

I hope in this book to encourage people to explore language more fully through *both* the spoken and the written word, and to consider the various types of speech within their own language and beyond it. This is a process that requires a great deal of energy, but not a great deal of expenditure – it is a non-consumerist activity. We need to get back to "linguistic health" by exercising our linguistic abilities with the same obsessiveness that we currently apply to trimming up our bodies. For millennia we have been oppressed by work; now we are oppressed by our redundancy in relation to a technological economy that provides for us and entertains us in accordance with an alien logic. I am not a Luddite, but I believe we have to learn to live with modern technology in a more modest manner that suits our natures and our planet, not business or technology itself. Our children's linguistic education in the school and at home has to become more demanding, and this will produce more balanced adults capable of dealing with our tremendous challenges. Language and politics are inextricably mixed. But I do not wish to imply that the monoglot adult has no hope, and language learning is certainly not the only way to develop our linguistic abilities – but it remains an extremely effective one.

Let me end then with an anecdote from my childhood which may have affected my thinking or perhaps illustrates how that thinking had already been changed. At some stage in my early boarding career, there were a few French boys over briefly as part of a school exchange, and I can very clearly see them now in a huddle as they happily chattered in their native tongue. My own school companions grumpily complained that the visitors didn't need to speak French, as they spoke English very well, and I seem to remember that they did in fact have a serviceable although halting command of the language. In monoglot England of the late fifties and early sixties, English was the natural language of humanity and speaking anything else a kind of affectation. I failed in my attempt to explain that that was *their* language, the one *they* were at home in. I understood this not because I was more intelligent than the other boys, but because I too had stood in a place where I didn't belong and felt the exhilaration of being amongst difference, which for me had been a challenge not a threat. I understood what the French boys were experiencing and was even a little envious. Learning languages as a child is a simple and natural process;

learning languages as an adult is an extremely difficult and humiliating experience that initially reduces you down to a command of language that is worse than childlike. But the pain is worthwhile, as it brings rewards that cannot really be explained to those who have not experienced them. It brings you parallel lives and a fuller sense of what it means to be human.

Allan Cameron, Sulaisiadar, Isle of Lewis, 2007

In Praise of
Garrulous

Chapter One

Silence, like gold, is the currency of the powerful

The nurse entered the children's ward and put her straightened and upright index finger to her pursed lips. The children, although sick, were linked by a chain of hushed discourse and suppressed giggles. "Silence is golden," she said. Their natural exuberance slowly died, like a suffocation. Heads crashed down on pillows by an act of will. Some puffed their disapproval as they turned on their sides. Her act was the expression of a smug culture that believes it already possesses every truth that is of any worth and has nothing else to say. Talking is for time-wasters and trouble-makers. Silence is for stability and for the knowledge that every-thing is in its proper place and everybody at their proper rank. She switched the room into darkness.

Talkativeness is something that varies greatly from one cul-ture to another, but throughout all cultures there appears to be a tendency for the wealthy and powerful, in spite of their greater leisure, to talk less than the poor and powerless. Men too are generally more silent than women, and adults more silent than children. The only cases in which the powerless go silent are those in which the powerful decide to batter them into the muteness of beasts. These are the extreme cases of the army, the prison and the concentra-tion camp. This is the shuffling misery of regimentation, but however much they attempt to mangle and mould the mass, its constituent individuals always manage to mutter their

way back to their human origins. They utter their unique-
ness under their breath, which condenses in the cold air of
the parade ground or prison yard. Words, which are given
to us by history and society, are the means by which we distinguish ourselves from history and society, and they allow
us to become individuals. Individuality, then, is the product
of a mass convention, a shared system of signs called language. Individuality, so often contrasted with society, is in
fact its product. Or put most simply, without society there is
no individuality, whereas the modern concept of economic
individualism which is supposed to transcend society is in
fact no more than consumerist conformism.

The powerful do not speak, because speaking means
opening yourself up and putting yourself on the same level
as the person you are speaking to. A true dialogue – the idea
of the dialogue – presupposes complete equality. In reality,
conversations, particularly short ones, often reflect social
relations. One person may express superiority in his delivery,
while the other person may talk back in a manner that either
accepts or rejects that claimed superiority. A supplicant will
approach his patron with deference in the hope of obtaining
his request, and the patron may answer in a manner that
enhances his reputation for magnanimity, as he wrestles
between his need not to give too much away and his need
to feel the power of his generosity. Ultimately, you arrive at
the command, where one person asserts his complete control over the other, and expects little more than a "yes, sir" in
response. But real sustained conversation requires equality,
and that is where we express our characters most fully and
accept the humanity of others. Speaking is therefore both a
subversive act and a collective means of testing and developing our thoughts. The further up the social hierarchy a
person is, the fewer the people with whom he can engage in
dialogue without subverting his own position. This factor,

which could be defined as the isolation of power, is a product of the need for the powerful to present an image that reflects and justifies the power they hold. If Bakhtin was right in claiming that carnival was a social reversal in which the "barriers of caste, property, profession and age" were temporarily removed, then it must have been as much of a release for the powerful as it was for the powerless.

Speaking involves us exposing ourselves. It means putting our arguments in the public domain. As all our arguments are necessarily flawed, because it is never entirely possible to take into account all the various shifting realities that could affect them, we are leaving ourselves open to valid counter-arguments and in some cases to ridicule. It takes courage to speak, and even greater courage to speak out against the flow of conformity.

Because the powerless are more generous in their assessments of their fellow human beings, they judge the silently powerful to be intelligent but unwilling to engage in dialogue with their intellectual inferiors, perhaps even out of a sense of propriety or a desire not to embarrass their underlings with a show of powerful thought. For the most part, they are wrong: the silence of the powerful generally hides the vacuousness of the strong. The powerful, on the other hand, are much less charitable. For them, both the silence and the garrulousness of the weak are a sign of bestiality, stupidity and even imbecility. They too are mostly wrong. They are more acquainted with the silence of the weak, as that silence can be a sign of justifiable fear or prudence, and a desire not to engage in a battle in which all the social weapons are held by one side only. In every case, silence has an air of menace, because it keeps everyone else in a state of ignorance as to the nature that hides behind that silence.

An old Tuscan saying states that "Every fool is a sage when he keeps his mouth shut" ("Ogni pazzo è savio quando tace").

5

Many a professor defeats a dangerously bright undergraduate not by superior arguments and experience but by staring silently and fixedly over a pair of half-glasses. The ferment of the youth's ideas is no match for the calm certainty and emptiness of the professor's hubris.

There is one case in which the powerful speak and the powerless remain silent, and that is in the formal setting of an address by a powerful figure to the crowd. The powerful always believe those beneath them to be a crowd; that is why they call them a mass. By becoming a mass, individuals abdicate all individuality and act as the caricature that the powerful want them to be. The crowd is featureless, but attains a degree of power, however temporary, precisely because it is a crowd and has abdicated all individual responsibility. For this reason the powerful deign to address the crowd with respect, while they would treat each of its individual members with disdain.

Silence has mystery, and mystery has power. This is reason enough for not speaking about oneself to those of inferior rank. Again popular wisdom provides a clear awareness of this reality: "familiarity breeds contempt" and "no man is a hero to his valet (or wife)". The latter expression applies the former one to a social reality. A "hero" is generally a man and of a certain class, and therefore exercises power in relation to his sex and his class. These sayings, perhaps unconsciously, express an important truth: power is an act and the powerful are actors, and thus anyone who is constantly backstage will be unable to find the performance convincing. The proximity of servants was one of the most terrible sufferings of the rich until the eighteenth century when architecture and technological advances made it possible to put some distance between the smell of the rich and the smell of the poor.

Language and the lack of language (or in other words,

loquaciousness and taciturnity) are therefore tools to hide ourselves from the world. We create a mask with them, and then with varying degrees of success we conceal our real self behind it. We only reveal ourselves, not always through language, to those we feel close to. It is not simply a matter of power, although it is also that, because we are more likely to reveal ourselves to those we consider to be similar to ourselves. In the simplified sociological reality of our own times, these barriers are beginning to disappear, and we speak of personal matters more indiscriminately, sometimes to the point of indulging in a deaf and deafening self-obsession.

The contrast between silence and talkativeness does not merely concern power and the lack of it; it also concerns the type of society in which the language community lives. A feudal monarchy talked in a different way from a mercantile republic, and a modern capitalist state talks in a different way from a socialist or a pre-capitalist state. The Italian republics that came under pressure from the great European monarchies in the sixteenth century despised the servile language of the latter. Of course they had class too, and this was reflected in their speech, but they did not address people as *vossignoria* (your lordship), nor did they say, *le bacio le mani* ("I kiss your hands"). A more profound distinction can be found in the rise of the bourgeoisie (if I may use so dated a term), because this class preferred a more direct approach to language, and the English language was at the forefront of this change. The bourgeoisie (and let's be clear that I am talking primarily about a class that believed in hard work and engaged in trade or a trade) tended in very general terms to think in linear and utilitarian terms. Speech, like most things, had to justify its existence and therefore became less elaborate. The structure of language shifted in relative terms from hypotaxis to parataxis (from complex forms such as subordinate clauses, appositional clauses, reversals of word order, etc. to simple forms, ultimately a concatenation of main clauses joined by the most commonly used conjunctions "and" and "but"), and the structure of argumentation shifted from the examination of the peripheral arguments working towards the principal argument or thesis, to the examination of the principal argument or thesis to which peripheral arguments could be added as a kind of optional backup. These trends have not been reversed in consumer society, in spite of increased leisure; they have progressed even further and spread to all sections of society.

Modernity has thus involved an increase in silence or rather human taciturnity because, overall, society has become much noisier as the speaker with a larynx has been replaced by the speaker with a transducer. While a typical public space would once have been full of the noise of the human voice, it is now often the case that the electronically produced human voice makes conversation impossible. What has not been destroyed by the clockwatching of industrialisation and Taylorism has been drowned out by muzak and broadcasting – the monotonous rhythm of recycled music and the mindless chatter suited to everyone and therefore nobody. The great Bosnian writer, Ivo Andrić, believed that the advent of the radio in the first decade of the twentieth century would destroy the pleasure of conversation and the ability to make one's own entertainment. This Nobel Prize-winner lived until 1975 and would therefore have known how prescient were the words in his masterpiece, *The Bridge over the Drina*. Since his death, however, it has become possible to plug one's brain into a Walkman, i-pod or MP3, which presumably not only impedes conversation but also blots out the dialogues we have in our brains. But thankfully the West is not all the world (and within the West there are significant variations). One sociolinguist tells us with slightly suspect certitude that the most garrulous linguistic group in the world is the Roti tribe of East Timor.[1] Until the Indonesian bombs rained down on them with the connivance of some western powers, they must have been a lucky people indeed, and they must have had leisure to have gained so prized a laurel.

The swing from hypotaxis to parataxis and from garrulous-ness to taciturnity is not however new, but it is more extreme than in the past. Plato was basically arguing for a rejection of rhetoric or excessive rhetoric.[2] His thinking was linear and plain, and this added to its force. His language must have been particularly potent when all around people were using something more elaborate. None of these forms are prefer-able in absolute; they only become preferable within a social context. Machiavelli used an extremely powerful direct and paratactical language, typical of republican Florence. It was a language that was destined to disappear, and has never fully returned. However, these forms of language can do dif-ferent things. Parataxis has the advantage of being able to present a very clear logical sequence, but hypotaxis has the advantage of being able to run different logical sequences, sometimes contradictory ones, at the same time.

Language is not simply about logic and reason; it is also a means to act directly upon another's emotions and, if success-ful, to take possession of their brains and manipulate them. Just as animals in a pack strut, threaten and entice, so their human relations do the same with an added weapon in their

1 . John McWhorter, *The Power of Babel. A Natural History of Language* (London: Heinemann, 2002), p. 9. The Roti "process silence as downright threatening and appear to talk a mile a minute." They seem as exotic as the Hyperboreans were to the Greeks, but whatever the exaggeration, the underlying point is valid: loquaciousness varies greatly from one society to another.
2 . Plato was not above parody and playing with style. In *Phaedrus*, Socrates says to his companion, "Haven't you noticed, bless you, that I have become not merely lyrical but actually epic, as if the former weren't bad enough?" (Harmondsworth: Penguin Classics, 1973), p. 42.

armoury: language. When someone speaks, they are also a physical presence (male or female, young or old, attractive or ugly, prosperous or impoverished, threatening or meek). The voice, too, has or lacks persuasive elements. It can be smooth and assured or it can be tremulous and uncertain. Anyone with experience of the world should know that the speaker with the latter kind of voice is generally more reliable than the former, and yet our instinct is always to trust the former. Even the most unscrupulous manipulators of the former are themselves likely to be victims of their own wiles, such is the power of this instinct.

Spoken language is therefore created and interpreted within a context that includes many non-verbal elements. Listeners will vary in their ability to filter out the false logic, the sophistry and even the cruder weapons of menace and flattery, but no one is entirely immune to these manifest persuaders. Written language is, in this sense, pure language. It is deprived of the writer's presence and is recreated from the page by the reader's will. Readers might imagine the author's voice (or voices) and recreate accent and tone within their heads, but they are in control. Written language is less democratic because, for most of history, access has been restricted to an elite, but it is more democratic because it is less susceptible to manipulation. Clearly, the greater is the percentage of readers within a society, the greater the democratic influence of writing. It could be argued that democracy is impossible or at least worthless without a literate and educated electorate that reads at least fairly regularly.

I will examine writing more fully in a later chapter, but here we are interested in it solely as pure language coming from a single source without any interruption except the one imposed by the reader's concentration. The spoken language is adulterated and modulated, as I have suggested throughout this chapter, by pauses and silences. The spoken language is anarchic in its every aspect: words are not naturally distinct phonetically, nor are sentences syntactically. A pause or a break in a sentence can signify a threat or display timidity according to the other somatic signals that accompany it. Writing instils order on the spoken language, whose order is never real but only implicit. Writing strips out not only facial expression, attitude, posture and all the other markers, but also the complex linguistic nuances of tone, pitch, accent and diction. No amount of descriptive adverbs can make up for this loss: "she cried angrily", "he paused in his utter confusion", "she sighed wearily", and so on. But the written word in its poverty survives as a powerful force because of its purity and its density. It has the power to oppress, but more particularly it has the power to subvert. It is pondered garrulousness.

The two extremes of talkativeness are the ritual conversation and the subversive one. Typical of the first category is talk about the weather, which is clear for all to see, but nevertheless provides a subject about which nobody has to think too much as they go about their business. This is a kind of verbal grooming whereby two or more individuals re-establish cordial relations. Content is of no or minimal importance. The apparently asinine nature of these exchanges conceals their subtlety: nuanced degrees of warmth or coolness mark out the relationship between two animals. Typical of the second category is humour, which has its own internal, sometimes cruel logic. To be witty occasionally means saying or implying things you do not necessarily believe. It can be crude and brutal, and in those cases often little more than a pugnacious assertion of prejudices. But at its best, humour is complex and helps us to see and interpret reality in new ways. Good humour attacks the commonplace, and is therefore inherently subversive.

Writers and readers are attracted by the purity of language and its rational elements, but they should not forget its many other functions, particularly in its spoken form: language is about structuring power within human society, it is about storing a society's knowledge, it is about cataloguing and defining ownership in the widest possible sense of the term, it is a form of caressing, it is an enjoyment in itself, it is a musical instrument. Language is almost everything we are: it governs our existence, and the fact that we are now more aware of our closeness to other animals only increases our awe for this almost miraculous facility that in some ways transcends biology and ourselves, and goes in search of reason. Its origins are unknown and possibly unknowable, but speculations on them, however idle, have the merit of clarifying some of the problems.

Chapter Two

The birth of language

Pressure built up within an enormous Mind, as we shall call the wordless entity of concentrated energy and matter that we can never know and still less understand. One day before days of any length existed, It exploded and propelled Its fragments of energy and matter on many different trajectories over distances that make distance incomprehensible. But it was cold – cold and silent – in the endless expansion into nothingness. Exploding stars brought little comfort to the Mind who worried about His existence and changed Himself from neuter to masculine in an effort to feel His being. "I am a set of rules," He said at last, "a set of physical rules that must be obeyed, but do I exist if no one can understand those rules or even be aware that they might exist?

"I must allow the random creation of a solar system in which one planet can allow the random collision of amino acids which will allow the random development of animal life which will allow the eventual development of what I really want: an animal that can speak. And if that animal can speak, it will be able to think and from its tiny perspective develop an understanding, a little understanding of my set of rules. But I will play a game with it, so that every time it discovers a rule, that little piece of knowledge will spawn a thousand more perplexities and unsolved riddles, thus keeping it in a constant state of excited ignorance."

And so it came to pass. The Mind heard the animals speak, and saw that it was good. They called up to him with many words, "God, Gott, Deus, Dio, Dia, Allah, Yahweh," and thousands upon thousands of other names. Some believed He was one thing and some another. They fought amongst themselves not only over what the nature of the Mind might really be, but simply over what name to give Him. We cannot say how the Mind responded. If He was full of love, then He would have been saddened that His work had come to this end. If He was full of power, He would have rejoiced that His signs and wonders had multiplied in the land of the talking animals.

Some divided over a filioque, some divided over the number of fingers they used in an act of deference to the Mind. And the Mind saw that it was not so good. In order to be and absolutely fulfil His essence, the Mind needed to be understood by the little creatures that scurried and chattered on the remote planet He had chosen for them, and yet He now had to admit that language not only leads to better understanding but also to wilful misunderstanding.

In linguistics there is no "creation" theory that has an equivalent authority to the theory of evolution in biology; there is not even a convincing working hypothesis that gives us some idea of how this wonderful ability came about and how it defines our human nature. Instead we have a fairly wretched parliament of pseudo-scientific dreamers who expatiate earnestly with little reference to the enormity of the speculative task they have undertaken. Sociolinguistics has made considerable progress in recent decades both in recording language as a social phenomenon and in attempting to develop a theory of language and of what languages can and cannot do.[1] The problem for those who wish to trace language back to a supposed origin is that language before writing left no trace. The bones and artefacts of early

---

1. It could be argued that the effect of Chomsky's "generative grammar" on language has been as revolutionary as that of Darwin's theory of evolution on our perception of what humanity is. Each theory is an enormous leap forward, and has to be taken as a starting point for further investigations. This does not mean they are entirely unassailable, because science will always refine its knowledge. However, Chomsky's principal theory does not concern the origins of language, for which there is still no persuasive hypothesis.

man may survive, but his words were like dried leaves and crumbled to dust under the heavy tread of pre-history when man – "primitive man" – was few in number and subject to his environment rather than master of it. We have no reason to believe that he was more stupid than us or that, once he had fully gained his linguistic tool, he was less articulate. In fact, it may well have been the other way round.

John McWhorter, the author of a sociolinguistic compendium for public consumption and therefore a general overview of the current state of play, confidently asserts that human language started with just one language, which is predictably called the Ur-language. Scientifically we have no way of knowing whether or not there was only one original human language or how such a language could have come about. As it is hard to believe that the extraordinary linguistic skills of human beings were born "all of a piece", it seems just as likely that some rudimentary form of independent language (not hard-wired) was already in existence before the self-appointed *homo sapiens* developed as a species. It is then equally likely that language differentiated itself linguistically but not biologically before a recognisably complex human language appeared – that language skills grew in an environment of linguistic diversity and flexibility through an evolutionary process that pre-dated our current languages and our emergence as a finite species.

Only a very loose grammatical template and the ability to learn language is hard-wired. It appears to be in the nature of language to fragment and evolve quickly, and this process was only reversed by the rise of the state, which imposes greater uniformity spatially, and writing, which slows down the rate of change (and imposes greater uniformity chronologically). We have, of course, no way of knowing because the history of language starts with all the rest of human history; it is written history and the writing down of older oral history that marks out history from the gloom of pre-history. Recently archaeology has taken us a little further back, but mainly it has added to our knowledge of periods on which written records had already thrown some light. The most sensible comments on the origins of language are in my opinion the self-confessed speculations of Bruce Chatwin in his book *Songlines*, which considers the origins of language principally in relation to the aboriginal peoples of Australia. The dialogue between the policeman and Arkady, the Russo-Australian champion of the Aborigines, is undoubtedly one of the most powerful scenes in the book:

> Many Aboriginals, [Arkady] said, by our standards would rank as linguistic geniuses. The difference was one of outlook. The whites were forever changing the world to fit their doubtful vision of the future. The Aboriginals put all their mental energies into keeping the world the way it was. In what way was that inferior?[2]

"Primitive" peoples are polyglots, poets, songsters and taxonomists. Lacking intellectual specialisms, they can boast a much wider knowledge of the human arts and the environment that surrounds them. Chatwin was particularly interested in the close relationship between language and landscape, and the use of song to memorise the topography of aboriginal itineraries. If this is correct, then oral hunter-gatherer societies must have attempted to retain the integrity of their stories while allowing their languages to change, in part through the inevitable instability of the non-literate and in part through their attempts to improve on their poetry. Modern societies change the storylines in a constant

---

2. Bruce Chatwin, *Songlines* (London: Vintage, 2005; first publication Jonathan Cape, 1987), pp. 123-4.

search for new material that shocks and titillates, but show less interest in language itself, which so often fails to rise above the most pedestrian mimesis.

Steven Pinker provides a very interesting example of the complexity and subtlety of languages in societies once considered primitive or even "savage" by European imperialism: the highly agglutinate language, Kivunjo, which is spoken in Tanzania and Kenya, has an extremely complicated tense structure; indeed there are tenses that refer the action of a verb to today, earlier today, yesterday, no earlier than yesterday, yesterday or earlier, the remote past, the habitual, the ongoing, the consecutive, the hypothetical, the future, an indeterminate time and the occasional. Moreover, it has various markers, including the prefix "n-" which indicates that the word is the "focus" of that particular part of the conversation. I will make more of this point when I examine what I define as the Social Mind, but for the moment let us stress that "primitive" man in historical times generally uses complex linguistic forms, and it is therefore legitimate to conjecture that early man also did. This point is relevant here because it relates to how language is perceived in the definition of man.

Dante, who obviously believed that all animals were created by God and did not change or evolve, did however believe in a hierarchy that developed from the basest animals, made a gigantic leap to mankind and then another gigantic leap to angels. Language, for him, defined the human being and its intermediate place.[3] Darwin, who obviously believed in evolution, also believed in evolution within the human species. He was certainly not Gobineau, but his ideas did reflect most of European thinking at the time (imperialism) and he perceived gradations that continued from the animal

---

3. Dante Alighieri, *De vulgari eloquentia*, Latin and Italian bilingual text (Milan: Garzanti, 1991), p. 7.

kingdom into humanity. To some extent there has been a partial return to this thinking. Those who hold these views naturally want to downplay the importance of language and give greater importance to technological advancements (it may of course be that Darwin as a biologist felt more qualified to speak about the other factors). He clearly states, "[Language] certainly is not a true instinct, for every language has to be learnt." But he is clearly confused, because he immediately backtracks and claims that "man has an instinctive tendency to speak, as we see in the babble of our young children."[4] He needed to show how his evolutionary continuum went through many gradations that divide both animals and men:

> Nor is the difference slight in moral disposition between a barbarian, such as the man described by the old navigator Byron, who dashed his child on the rocks for dropping his basket of sea-urchins, and a Howard or a Clarkson; and in intellect, between a savage who uses hardly any abstract terms, and a Newton or Shakespeare. Differences of this kind between the highest of men of the highest races and the lowest savages, are connected to the finest gradations. Therefore it is possible that they might pass and be developed into each other.[5]

We now know more about "primitive" languages and are not so dismissive of them (indeed we admire their complexities).[6] But what matters here is that by considering

---

4. C. Darwin, *The Descent of Man and Selection in Relation to Sex* (Akron Ohio: The Werner Company, 1874), p. 87.

5. *The Descent of Man ...*, p. 66.

6. If Darwin had read Wilhelm von Humboldt's *Linguistic Variability and Intellectual Development*, he would have discovered that the complexity of "primitive" languages was already known.

language to be the main determinant of what it is to be human we are also compressing the whole of humanity onto the same stage in evolution, and marking out the distinctiveness of its separation from other animals (evolution does appear to be a series of steep climbs and plateaus, so this human plateau is not an unusual occurrence). In this sense, the recognition of the importance of language in our nature is a humanism, and takes us back to the humanist tradition that straddled the Middle Ages and the Early Modern Era. For English-speakers, Hamlet's soliloquy immediately springs to mind.[7] But of course, when we now argue that language, rather than the more mundane opposable thumb or bipedalism, is the badge of our distinctiveness, and that we are therefore divided by culture and not biology or divine intervention, we are not denying our closeness to the animals; we are simply indicating the particular gift of nature and evolution that has ensured our survival and perhaps made us dangerously successful.

The opposable thumb allows us – alone amongst the primates – to get a really good mechanical grip on the world around us, while language has enabled us to express our individuality and to communicate with others in great depth. It has nurtured our reflective side and allowed us to store up knowledge. The hand with an opposable thumb has allowed us to grasp the sword, battle-axe, spear and dagger. It set us on the path of war. As technology developed, the contributions of the two attributes became more balanced. The opposable thumb made it possible to hold a pen and record language, and language became a tool of power and class differentiation. Together these two remarkable attributes have

---

7. "What a piece of work is a man! How noble in reason! how infinite in faculty! in form, in moving, how express and admirable! in action how like an angel! in apprehension how like a god! the beauty of the world! the paragon of animals!" *Hamlet* (1601). Act 2, Scene 2, l.

allowed the construction of all the great machinery of coercion that surrounds us – coercion that affects us and affects our entire environment.

I have heard that dolphins too might have the faculty of language expressed through the modulation of their clicking sounds. If this is true, they are extremely fortunate not to have a hand with an opposable thumb. Perhaps they have languages and dialects. Perhaps they recite poetry to each other in the South Atlantic while one of their number simultaneously translates it into White Sea for the benefit of a delegation from the north. But no one can lift a weapon and no one can impose their will. So dolphins leap from the waves, and humans toil and look on jealously at a talented species that does not appear to have been expelled from its earthly paradise. We feel an affinity but also feel that we came off worse in our airy element than they did in their watery one.

We may be inclined to adopt attitudes of moral superiority in relation to men like Darwin, but we are all affected by the spirit of our time, often to the detriment of our own ideas (and of no one more than Darwin could it be said that he was not affected by the *zeitgeist* but, rather, invented it). It must have been very difficult for Western Europeans, like any other people who finds itself militarily unstoppable, not to believe in their own innate superiority and to translate that false sense of superiority into exceptionally cruel behaviour. It could be argued that they were less cruel than many other peoples who found themselves temporarily in such a position and whose reputation relies on myth as much as it does on historical fact: the Vandals, the Huns and the Mongols (whose orgies of destruction annihilated cities and brought to an end the advanced civilisations of the Middle East and Central Asia, and ultimately left the way open to the decline of the Arab world and its maritime empires and to the rise of Western Europe and its rival ones). But to put that argument, we would have to conceal (or continue to conceal) the unpalatable truths of what the Europeans did in sub-Saharan Africa in relatively recent times, for which there is ample documentation: the most hidden of the hidden holocausts. Another reason for European superiority was that the Victorians, who suffered in many ways from their Industrial Revolution, were winning a battle that was as old as settled communities – the battle against our own dirt. Today, after the terrible events of the twentieth century, one would have hoped that no sane person could insist upon the moral and intellectual superiority of the European.

But this quasi-moral humanist argument is not what primarily concerns me here, although it is a very valid and attractive one; I believe that the importance of language in defining human nature, which stresses the underlying similarities and therefore equality between all human beings irrespective of their material wealth, raises the question of how our unusual treatment of language has been affecting the people of the West for some time and is now beginning to affect nearly all the peoples of the world. I wish to argue that our current relationship with language is having some damaging effects on humanity as a whole or, at the very least, that this hypothesis deserves consideration.

McWhorter argues that his single primeval language "was low on decorative bells and whistles", and "that the first language, not having existed for a long enough time for inflections to appear through grammaticalisation or other gradual processes, can be assumed not to have had inflections".[8]

---

8. J.H. McWhorter, *The Power of Babel* ..., p. 301. McWhorter claims to have a fairly good idea about the first language spoken by man, the Ur-language, although he is wisely sceptical about attempts to reconstruct this as a "Proto-World", and modestly admits "we will never know its words". Given that his

If we go back just quarter of a century, learned thinking appears to have been even more bizarre: Ronald Englefield is absolutely certain that, while language was undoubtedly a remarkable "invention" on the part of humanity, it was "no more remarkable than the fact that apes do not make use of bows and arrows, clothes or agricultural implements".[9]

These speculations are less than convincing. Because we have fossil evidence, it appears that the brain of our fore-bears began to grow about 2.5 to 2.0 million years ago and ceased about 400,000-200,000 years ago. It may be assumed that at least in part that brain growth was needed to develop the power of speech, and that the power of speech required brain power to deal with a multiplicity of languages. This seems much more logical than the idea that the ability developed before the reality that required it, which is exactly what Englefield and McWhorter are arguing, the former very crudely and the latter in a more nuanced or, some might say, inconsistent manner.[10] As for the lack of ornamentation in early speech, it seems just as probable that ornamentation was precisely the element that drove language development. Our ancestors probably had more subtle minds and more time to chatter, to natter, to jabber, to gibber, to gabble, to gas, to prattle, to prate, to blather, to blether and to oth-erwise engage in that activity for which the English lan-guage has such an abundance of pejorative verbs. In other words, to dwell upon that God-given right and ability to be

---

accounts of the origins of Italian (pp.67-8) and Urdu (pp. 69-70) contain inac-curacies, I don't think we should take his extravagant claims too seriously.

9. R. Englefield, *Language. Its Origin and Relation to Thought* (London: Elek/Permberton, 1977), p. 2.

10. McWhorter says that he is open to the idea that language is not innate, but merely an invention or "graft" (*The Power of Babel* ..., p. 9), even though he rightly points out that "language is [just] as sophisticated in all human cultures and is thus truly a trait of the species, not a certain 'civilized' subset of the spe-cies" (p. 6).

garrulous. But the comic-strip version of our ancestors still pervades our thinking and portrays our earliest ancestors as cave-dwellers who have suddenly realised the potential for modulating their grunts. I find it more believable that modern man is moving swiftly to plain language, reduced vocabulary and an absence of memory (because language and memory are intimately entwined). Evidence from the family of Indo-European languages since the invention of writing shows a marked trend from the complex towards the simple. All these languages appear to have originally had three genders, but many are now reduced to two and English has managed some time ago to dispense with gender altogether. Indo-European languages once had dual verb forms, but only Slovenian has retained this subtlety (and it is now disappearing in the spoken language). Older languages have more complex but also more elegant syntax (although some might say more cumbersome). Their vocabularies are more subtle and the meanings of their words more influenced by context (the standardisation of modern "national" languages has undoubtedly assisted learning, but it naturally discards such apparently useless things as context-specific colours). Welsh and Gaelic, like Latin, have no single word for "yes" and "no", and express these concepts by using a construction based on the main verb in the question. Gaelic, unlike Latin, has not yet learned how to predicate the verb to be with a noun. The construction, "she is a teacher" is impossible; it has to be either "it is a teacher that is in her" (*'s e tè-teagasg a th'innte*) or "she is in her teacher" (*tha i na tè-teagasg*). Obviously this does not mean that either Latin or Gaelic are unable to express certain subtleties; it means that Latin and Gaelic speakers work a bit harder and their linguistic abilities may therefore be more highly developed than those of speakers of newer and simpler languages. Of course, McWhorter could quite reasonably object that this example only concerns the very end of the long history of human language, but as the long prehistory remains in the dark and probably always will, he has no evidence other than the "common-sense" conceit that man is always evolving.

Englefield is more disconcerting in his claims (McWhorter's at least have the merit of a certain speculative logic). The inventions of clothing and agricultural implements denote cognitive abilities, which include language, or to put it another way, we are able to invent these things precisely because we have language. Moreover, language denotes a specific predisposition particularly in young children. Babies apparently lie on their backs for their first nine months showing few signs of activity because they are engaged in the difficult task of distinguishing and recording the pho-nemes specific to their own language community. What, we may ask, were they doing before language was "invented" or developed its complexities, if language came after our full development as a species? Other mammals are up and run-ning around the place long before that, because they do not have this difficult task imposed on them *by nature*. When Darwin was asked to specify the years in which humans do most of their learning, he replied with the surprising intui-tion of a scientific genius, "The first three."[11] Human beings are not capable of inventing their own brain; it is their brain that invents, and their brain already includes language as an essential component. After Chomsky, it has become clear that the human brain is designed to receive language. Humanity did not invent language; language invented or at least defined humanity.

I could find many examples of creation narratives for lan-guage other than my own modern version at the beginning

11. Quoted in Otto Jespersen, *Language: Its Nature, Development and Origin* (London: George Allen and Unwin, 1922), p. 103.

of this chapter. These myths are entirely harmless as long as they make no claim to be anything other than myths. When they dress themselves up as science and claim to be facts, they risk taking us off on a path of mistaken certitudes. Often when writers invent a creation myth, they are trying to say something about their contemporary society and beliefs. The desire for creation myths is perhaps itself a product of the template of human language: a subject acts upon an object, and so reality is a chain of cause and effect. The imagination then applies itself to that logic and comes up against the terrifying realisation that there must have been a first cause, just as there will ultimately be a final effect (today, we possibly do not see this as an inevitable truth). The first cause therefore obsesses the philosophical mind and provides the political thinker with a means to describe what he considers to be "natural", because the first cause is considered to be appropriate and very often divine, while everything that followed was some kind of degeneration or compromise with reality.

At least, this was the case up until the birth of the idea of progress, and even after that, large popular movements such as socialism and feminism continued to invent "golden ages" that could be reinvented in modern society. I cannot say whether Plato really believed that first man grew out of the ground and did not have a penis or indeed a female companion. I suspect that he didn't. However, he definitely believed in the primacy of men in relation to women and that sexual activity is a distraction from man's true nature, which is supposed to be meditative and rational. The myth was not a quirky little fable, a Tolkien-like reinterpretation of a form from a previous age primarily as a literary divertissement; it was a clear statement about the nature of pleasure, sex and man's place in the world. It is more likely but by no means certain that Rousseau believed his assertion that the first man who fenced off a piece of land was responsible for enslaving humanity. For us, of course, it is a much less outlandish claim; nevertheless the marking of a territory for agricultural use so that the sower of seed could enjoy the fruit of his or her labours some months later may well have been done not in the name of private property but communal ownership. Rousseau's creation myth for property is highly effective and personally I find the truth it suggests more appealing than Plato's wonderfully inventive but ultimately unacceptable pronouncements on sexual difference and the nature of pleasure. But I would advise against taking Rousseau's words too literally, as all myth is an over-simplification even at its best; ultimately Rousseau's words may well have been the force that emptied Phnom Penh.[12]

The best-known creation myth for language diversity is the Tower of Babel. The Old Testament tells the story in its typically succinct manner. After several verses listing the generations of Noah, it announces the plan to build a city and a tower:

> And the Lord came down to see the city and the tower, which the children of men builded. And the Lord said, Behold, the people is one, and they have all one language; and this they begin to do; and now nothing will be restrained from them, which they have imagined to do. Go to, let us go down, and there confound their languages, that they may not understand one another's speech. So the Lord

---

12. Please let me make it very clear to a more obtuse reader that I am not holding Rousseau responsible for the crimes of Pol Pot. His words provided an important line of enquiry and contain a truth. He cannot be blamed for their deification and the unfeeling fanaticism of those who turn myth and metaphor into certainty. Moreover, if these words have any moral responsibility, then we have to acknowledge the social goods they have produced as well as the social evils.

scattered them abroad from thence upon the face of the earth; and they left off to build the city.[13]

This myth falls into the category of arrogant assaults on the heavens – a cousin of the Titans' attack or that of Plato's cartwheeling hermaphrodite humans.[14] It is not a creation myth for language but for language diversity; its success, I think, is due to the fact that people have always tended to view language diversity as an unmitigated disaster. When linguistic fragmentation appeared an unassailable reality, it was perhaps sensible to dwell on the problems this creates. Now that wholesale language death has become an inevitability and the only question is the extent of the damage that will be inflicted, it is time to realise that linguistic diversity is essential to the survival of all languages, even the most powerful ones (see Chapter Five). Babel was to language what sex was to "men". According to Hesiod, the first woman, the frivolous, seductive and mendacious Pandora, opened the jar that contained all the anxieties and distressing cares of human existence, and the appearance of women and sex brought the golden age of men to an end.[15] We can up-end that myth and declare that the cloned men and the cloned language must have lacked all character, all subtlety, all menace, all love. Babel and Pandora released chaos on the world, and chaos, we now know, was the real creator of this world. Chaos may be brutal and stupid, but its random cross-fertilisation has always been the engine of evolution, even if we may not yet understand the mechanism perfectly.

Partly to show how our ideas on the origin of language have not developed a great deal over the centuries, I will examine Dante Alighieri's views on the subject (in contrast, our

---

13. Genesis, 11.5-8.
14. Plato, *The Symposium* (speech by Aristophanes), 190b-192e.
15. Hesiod, *Works and Days*, 60.

knowledge of language and language development in historical times has increased enormously). He, like McWhorter, took for granted that there was an Ur-language, and in *De vulgari eloquentia*, he declared that it was Hebrew.[16] In *The Divine Comedy*, however, his ideas had developed considerably. In *Paradise*, he states that the Adamic language was dead long before Nembroth built the Tower of Babel,[17] because of the *natural manner* in which our speech (*favella*) develops and diversifies, although he could not have got quite this far in the first canticle, as Nembroth in hell admits to his crime of splintering the single human language.[18]

Dante not only identified the natural tendency of language to fragment, he understood and perhaps exaggerated the rationalism that is inherent within it. Paradoxically, modern man, with all his conceits about his intellectual superiority, is more aware of the irrational characteristics that are intrinsic to language. However, if rationalism exists in the natural world, it must exist exclusively in humanity or, to be precise, in human language. Dante also understood that speech is mediated through the senses, and although he did not say as much in very explicit terms, it is the presence of this obligatory element that introduces the irrational and emotive characteristics of speech: its physical properties play upon our minds and influence our acceptance or rejection of rational propositions on the basis of non-rational criteria. To some extent he also understood this: "reason itself is differentiated between individuals according to their discernment, judgement and choices, so that everyone appears to enjoy their own particular type of reason".[19] But understanding through behaviour and sensations was, for him, strictly

---

16. Dante, *De vulgari eloquentia*, I, vi-vii (Milan: Garzanti, 1991), p. 13-19.
17. Dante, *Paradise*, XXVI, 124-6.
18. Dante, *Hell*, XXXI, 77-8.
19. Dante, *De vulgari eloquentia*, I, iii (Milan: Garzanti, 1991), p. 7.

for the animals, which are governed by instinct. Language was entirely the product of reason, and differentiation amongst human beings would therefore appear to have been a kind of hierarchy of reason, which no doubt reflected class as perceived in early fourteenth-century Tuscany.

Human reason is in any case firmly based on a logic developed through human storytelling. Language is based on a particular sequence: a subject acts upon an object or, more crudely, something does something to something else. Languages may order this sequence in dramatically different ways. Latin generally puts the verb at the end of the sentence (and cases allow it great flexibility with word order). Celtic languages always put the verb at the beginning of the sentence, and Gaelic generally follows the pattern: verb, subject, indirect object, direct object. English generally goes: subject, verb, object, indirect object. However, the logic remains the same, and the human mind appears to be hardwired to it (Chomsky). It is true that subordinate clauses can complicate sentence structure, but in a sense they only complement the main clause by reproducing its logic in relation to one of its elements. The basic human sentence is a story.

The exception to this logic is the verb "to be", which does not involve an action but rather an equivalence. Celtic languages prefer not to predicate the object on the subject using the verb "to be", as has already been shown (p. 23). It may be that the invention of the verb "to be" comes later, because then the sentence becomes a definition. And human reason can eventually go beyond human language, as in the case of complex mathematics. Language is not reason, but without language reason could not exist. Returning to Englefield's claim that language is an invention no more remarkable than "bows and arrows, clothes or agricultural implements", we could argue that he should have replaced "language" with "reason", but once again we have no way of knowing at what stage in our evolution reason became significant. Reason, at least in its purest form, is probably something that is taught, whereas language is universal to human beings and only absent in the event of some quite serious brain damage, physical disability or exclusion from society.

This leads us to the link between the two most important *natural* or *innate* activities of humanity that are unique to humanity: walking and talking. The human body is designed for walking and for walking in an extremely elegant manner compared with other animals that can at least temporarily lift themselves up on their back legs. Walking is so natural that it gives pleasure, and the absence of walking in our modern lives may be one of the motives for that nagging doubt that haunts the West: "Why are we, who are more affluent than any people in the past, not happier than we are?" Walking has a rhythm to it, and brings a pleasant calm. We enjoy walking in company and we enjoy walking alone. Language is another almost incessant activity in our lives, and even when we are not talking or listening, we engage in the internal dialogues or monologues that fill our days. Occasionally a newspaper will present us with statistics on how many hours in an average life we spend shaving, brushing our teeth or sitting on the lavatory, and the implication is that those moments are entirely lost. Such views, which reflect the dominant culture since Frederick Taylor started to order our actions, lose sight of the fact that when we engage in activities of this kind, we are also thinking. Inactivity and habitual activities serve a purpose: they allow us to let our minds run free, and this activity helps us to order our thoughts and prepares us for the more complex interactions we will have to confront in other moments of our day.

To deprive a human being of his or her ability to think in language by imposing a sequence of possibly very undemanding but rapid actions over an extended period of time is surely damaging, just like depriving someone of other human company over an extended period of time (solitary confinement). It may not be as damaging, but it certainly forces the human brain into a pattern of activity for which it was not designed. Tradesmen in the early American car industry must have been aware of this, as Ford had to double the skilled rate before he could attract workers to his unskilled posts Marx, whose methodology was supposed to be "scientific" just like Taylor's, developed his theory of alienation within the confines of economic theory, but the real problem is anthropological: the idea of what brings pleasure to human beings and engenders psychological health, and how much these should be offset against material gains. The answer to that question is one that has philosophical, religious and economic implications that go far beyond the matters under discussion. Here we will restrict ourselves to the following *hypothesis*: language is an activity for which the human body is designed (as ultimately the brain is part of the body) and its exercise is essential to our physical and psychological wellbeing, in a way that many other activities we consider important are not.

Of course, conversation is the most important forum for language, because language is learnt through hearing and then through talking. But as I have already suggested, real spoken language occurs within a social context that also reflects power relations between individuals. It can therefore be either stressful or relaxing. True dialogue, in which the interlocutors exchange stories and ideas, is of course one of the most satisfying activities in which human beings can engage. Sadly it is not so easy to achieve, at least in our society, and this too may be one of our problems. Today we don't converse, we network. Conversation is not a pleasure in itself, but a means to achieving ambitions and wealth. That, of course, is an exaggeration, because patently some people do enjoy networking and would find rambling dialogue without an agenda or fixed purpose an excruciating waste of time. Networking is not as new as the word itself, as literature particularly from the nineteenth century provides plenty of examples. Besides, people enjoy the company of others who have shared interests and knowledge: there is an intermediate position. On the other hand, Adam Smith claimed that even social gatherings of people from the same profession could lead to a plot against the public, and it could be added that they will often be as dull as detergent and dirty dishes soaked in water. The conversation will be about rivalry, and the company in which careers are made and lost is not for most people very relaxing. In reality, there are many types of dialogue, and most dialogues are hybrid and full of pleasant and unpleasant surprises. Dialogue within the brain, which might be called "reflective" dialogue, is also satisfying, but it is not true dialogue because one mind has control over both or all voices. However, it is also an ideal dialogue, as are all things imaginary.

The analogy between talking and walking is particularly pertinent because they are not only similar in their centrality to who we are, but appear to stimulate each other. Thinking, with its need to separate itself from the body by turning the body over to an instinctive activity, stimulates a desire to walk, and walking, with its rhythmic maximisation of all the body's activities, stimulates a desire to think. Bruce Chatwin was convinced that walking had similar psychological benefits to those I have attributed to thought (the exercise of language). He considered sedentary life to be the cause of our neurosis:

> The Bushmen, who walk distances across the Kalahari, have no idea of the soul's survival in another world. "When we die, we die," they say.

"The wind blows away our footprints, and that is the end of us."

Sluggish and sedentary peoples, such as the Ancient Egyptians – with their concept of an after-life journey through the Field of Reeds – project on the next world the journeys they failed to make in this one.[20]

Given that throughout most of the history of mankind we were hunter-gatherers who were small in number and covered large territories, walking and talking were probably our principal activities. As walking provides ample time for talking, the two activities might well have developed together. If this is the case, then the "unnatural" environment of the settled community has been a human problem for millennia, and our modern technological society is merely an exacerbation of the already inappropriate environment of the farm and the town, where humans were obliged to engage in isolated, repetitive and often back-breaking activities that radically reduced their favourite pastimes. Today, people can work in static, non-verbal realities, only to return home to the linguistically passive relationship with the box in the corner of the sitting-room. The neurosis of modern society might have a very long pedigree.[21]

Thus it is one of the premises of this essay that language is one of the principal or indeed the principal indicator of human nature. This attribute is so dominant that it cannot be some additional feature that developed after the advent of mankind, but was a complex and fully-developed capability that has existed in all human societies. As children have an innate ability to apply grammar and we therefore are

---

20. Bruce Chatwin, *Songlines*, p. 228.
21. I deal with the shift from the hunter-gatherer society to the settled, farming society in greater detail in my novel, *The Berlusconi Bonus*, 2005, pp. 113-5.

quite clearly designed to learn and use language, the title of Pinker's book – *The Language Instinct* – is, in this limited sense, entirely acceptable. Writing and reading are not an instinctive part of being a human being, but given the "language instinct", human beings have taken to them not like a duck to water (entirely instinctual), but perhaps like dolphins performing in a dolphinarium. Writing and reading place us in a somewhat artificial environment in which our natural talent can flourish. On the other hand, literature – whether oral or written (and don't tut-tut at the conflicting etymologies, as "oral literature" is now an accepted concept) – is an inherent feature not of every human individual, but certainly of every human society. My own speculation, based on no solid scientific evidence, is that oral literature in this wider sense must have been one of the drivers in the development of language before the fully developed *homo sapiens* appeared. Very possibly this occurred in the manner suggested by Chatwin: the pre-human societies that could better memorise landscape and taxonomy had a greater chance of survival, and this drove our forebear species towards humanity. No doubt many other cruder neo-Darwinian arguments could be formulated along the lines of linguistic excellence attracting a mate. Be that as it may, language is used by everyone and used in radically different ways. It is used by bletherers, pedants, manipulators, comics, poets and occasionally even by the taciturn. Even those who do not develop their linguistic skills very highly delight in hearing "bells and whistles" and the well-turned phrase. Language is not only a system of communication and an essential intellectual tool; it is, like music, highly accessible and capable of dramatically affecting the mood of the listener.

When I wrote the words "well-turned phrase", I immediately rejected it as a dead or at least very worn expression. I then thought that it did at least express the idea I wanted to put across: a well-crafted sentence that gives the feel of a smooth, perfectly shaped artefact that demonstrates skill and thought. But it doesn't. It actually suggests a well-*machined*, overly regular artefact from a limited range of possibilities. It is a cliché that describes cliché. I left it because it triggered my thoughts on McWhorter's "bells and whistles". Literary language that excites is a combination of content (there is an aesthetics of thought), sound, structure and presentation of the content (rhetoric or the aesthetics of speech) and, the most difficult concept of all, originality. All aesthetic judgements are a question of balance and made within a specific culture. What is considered well-judged rhetoric in one culture will be perceived as flowery or fussy in another. An idea may fascinate in one language community and be seen as either banal or over-complex in another.

If my definition of literary language is a reasonable approximation, then literature is possibly becoming less important in modern society. Today writing (whether for novels, television, film or theatre) is principally about extreme mimesis. I will discuss the disappearance of register later (Chapter Six), and that flattening out of language also affects the literary register – most particularly affects the literary register. We learn register just as we learn language, and we are designed to narrate through language. The decline in the entirely natural activity of oral literature and in written literature, which is much less natural but nevertheless very suited to our nature, has been paralleled by the rise in the very unnatural activity of narration through images, which requires the modern technology of film and television.

This poses an important question that I am clearly quite incapable of responding to, although my instinct is to support the affirmative answer: if language, its expert use, its diversity and its ornamentation are part of our natural being, are we damaged psychologically by being deprived of them?

This leads to a second question to which we can reply with some certainty: is a series of images capable of narrating the same moral complexities that a series of words can? Cinema is perhaps the greatest of the arts, if for no other reason than that it relies on the combined brilliance of so many people. In spite of this complexity of its production process and its involvement of nearly all our artistic sensibilities, it can never reproduce the complexity of, say, the novel, in which the reader can be *explicitly* introduced to the inner workings of each character's mind. A very typical example amongst the many is that of Milan Kundera's *The Unbelievable Lightness of Being*: the film was excellent as a film, but it fell far short of the book's power to evoke that pleasant sensation of bewilderment so essential to art and, in this particular case, the philosophical riddles which are the hallmark of Kundera's formidable writing skills. We are often more attached to our doubts than to our certainties, or at least we should be, because our doubts are more interesting. And the first question is the more interesting of the two. What I can establish is the complexity of our dependency on language, which at least favours an affirmative answer to that first question.

Chapter Three

Words are a gift from the dead

The elderly man screwed his monocle into his eye, examined the three sheets of typescript, and then threw them on the table. As he did so, he raised his eyebrow to release his monocle and thundered, "This is just psychobabble".

The face of the middle-aged man just opposite darkened and assumed a martyred look, while the young man to his left suppressed a flash of amusement that tugged at his lips and brightened his eyes. "Psychobabble, indeed", said the middle-aged man.

"Well, I agree", said the elderly man, still developing his own line of thought, "the author is quite a jolly cove, but he doesn't really explain anything about why the subject behaved in the way she did".

"Psychobabble, how dare you", said the middle-aged man, rising to the occasion.

"I mean, sir," said the elderly man with theatrical enjoyment, "that this study says nothing about the subject, and merely restates a series of tired old platitudes".

"Tired-old platitudes," said the young man almost under his breath as he attempted unsuccessfully to balance his silver fountain pen on the end of his index finger, "that platitude is getting a bit old and tired too".

"You mean. You mean," cried the middle-aged man; his voice swelled with his swelling anger, "I know exactly what a grotty little old man like you, with your ... with your absurd affectations of another age means by psychobabble".

"What do I mean?" said the elderly man, screwing his monocle back in and staring at the middle-aged man very coolly.

"Psychobabble, well ...," replied the middle-aged man, unnerved.

"Psychobabble", said the young man with an expression of sheer delight, "is a recently coined compound of 'psycho' from the Greek psyche for soul or butterfly, and 'babble' from the Middle English and similar to the Dutch babbelen and the French babiller with a possible reference to the Tower of Babel."

While the two other men stared at him, the silver fountain pen finally decided to balance itself on the end of his index finger, which took all his concentration.

So we are not born with a language but with something infinitely more wonderful: the ability to learn language. This obvious point has assumed a certain strangeness since the standardisation of language and the expansion of monolingualism have made language for many an almost fixed entity, often mistakenly associated with "ethnicity" which suggests a pseudo-biological connection.

Without language we cannot think. Without thought, Descartes would question our existence. Yet language comes to us from our own society and above all from history. A language contains not the history of a people but the history of its speakers. Speakers of the language in which I am writing are supposed to be an ethnic mix of a Germanic people and the indigenous Celts they found in the land they invaded (more probably it goes even further back and we are mainly derived from some pre-Celtic people or peoples). But most of the words I write are of not Anglo-Saxon but Latin origin. Moreover, the Latin words were not brought to England by speakers whose ancestors had spoken neo-Latin for many generations. They were brought by Norsemen, a Germanic people who had settled in the Land of the Franks, another

Latinised Germanic people who had learnt their language not from the Romans but from Latinised Celts. The language we speak does not reflect the history of a people, but rather the history of various European empires and migrations that occurred far from the shores of England. English is a European artefact created by events, some of which predated the arrival of the Angles and Saxons in Britain. If Hannibal had marched on Rome immediately after his stunning victory at Cannae, where Latins, Africans, Gauls and Iberians slogged away at the brutal business of battle in an exclusively Mediterranean war, then I might be writing in a predominately Semitic language; I would certainly not be writing in a Latinate one. The English imposed English on Ireland and on the rest of Britain, and then took it farther afield. An imperial language flattens all before it and so, after an initial period of increased linguistic activity and interchange, the variety of human thought and expression dwindles.

Words are the product of people and the use of language. They are the product of laziness, which elides consonants or twirls them in voiced and unvoiced couplets; they are the product of hard work and trade, which creates and imports new objects; they are the product of writers, who mould a language for a people when a culture is young; they are the product of the good humour and wisdom of a people, who collect the collective resistance of individuals through lives that are often short and unspeakably harsh; but above all they are the product of power, which both seeks to distinguish itself and encourages emulation.

Words are sound. Sound has its own colour, tone and rhythm. Sociolinguists say that no language is intrinsically more beautiful than another. There is perhaps some truth in that, but language is also capable of its own music and only humans can judge whether music is beautiful or not. Words are sounds for people, whose judgements may be distorted by social prejudice, but under that prejudice it is not entirely impossible that some general rules of human aesthetics have their own weight and influence.

Words come together to create meanings and ideas. Meanings and ideas can also have their own beauty. They can be plain or ornate. They can be complex or simple. But they cannot exist without language, so inevitably they are influenced by the language in which they are expressed.

The way we put meaning and ideas together is taught to us as part of our language. We are completely trapped within the strange and muddled history of our mother tongue, and we think within its confines. And yet this gift from millions of unknown speakers, who may have lived on the other side of the world, not only constrains us but also provides us with the means, the only means to become our own individual selves. Language reminds us of a fundamental fact that is easily forgotten in the consumer age: we can only express our individuality through our relationship with society. We are given words, but are free to use them and the infinite permutations they offer in a totally individualistic manner.

When we have a child, we create the inevitability of another death and the anxiety of a life lived in an imperfect and often brutally violent world. This sobering thought may depress us and if we pondered these considerations more often (instead of wilfully avoiding them), we might never have children again. As always, there are opposing lines of thought, and in this case less dismal ones. One thing we do by putting a child into this world is to trigger both the reciprocal use of language between our child and the other human beings it comes into contact with, as well as a more private "stream of consciousness". As the child grows and comes into contact with more people and diverse linguistic and social situations, he or she will develop a manner of speech that is entirely unique. In some cases, our child will grow up with a different language to our own, and there can be many reasons for this: migration, social climbing, language shift at community level, political change and war. In many cases, there will be a diglossic transition which could last for centuries. We are moulded by our linguistic past and shape the linguistic future, but we do so unconsciously, inadvertently and with very little control over the process, as often happens with the really important things in our lives.

Before the invention of writing, poetry was the collective memory that stored up history and knowledge. People must have savoured words and held onto their complexities which would often have had a mnemonic function, because words were not only to be expressed but also stored in the form of oral text. Modern languages are likely to be more succinct and, quite possibly have a greater stock of abstract nouns (I am ignoring here the question of scientific language, whose exponential increase is far beyond the reach of any single individual, as even scientists only know their own specialisms); ancient speakers would, of course, have had a greater command of the taxonomy of nature, as they lived closer to it.

Darwin was clearly wrong in assuming the simplicity of "savage" tongues, and in contrasting them with Shakespeare's (a sleight of hand and a shift of categories, because he is comparing languages unknown to him not with English but with English's greatest poet). However he also failed to understand the autonomy of language from the instinct to learn a language. The difference between the language of Shakespeare (itself a hybrid of current English and the Renaissance classical culture) and the language of the groundlings Shakespeare liked to ridicule was minuscule compared with the difference between "dumb animals" and those groundlings. These despised audiences were probably illiterate and had to engage in whatever backbreaking tasks Elizabethan society had allocated them, but their undoubted linguistic abilities (given that no society is voiceless) were such that they were willing to return to the theatre for some more gentle ribbing. They presumably wouldn't have done so, if they did not find the plays entertaining and comprehensible (in spite of the foreign words, foreign names and often distinctly Latinate syntax). Now we know just how complex language acquisition is in terms of the identification of phonemes, words, their meanings and the grammar that holds it all together, there can be no doubt that all human beings are born with not just a natural predisposition to the learning of language but also an all-consuming mental imperative to do so.

We should examine the nature of what Steven Pinker calls the "language instinct", and if this is just another name for Chomsky's theory of "transformational grammar", then the expression is probably a good one, but he gives the impression that he wants to take this argument one stage further. Pinker appears to belong to a growing, semi-religious movement of "ultra-Darwinists" whose high priest is Richard Dawkins. I have a feeling that if Darwin were alive today he would have recycled one of Marx's comments and said, "If these are Darwinists, then I am not a Darwinist." Evolution is an established scientific fact, and the haverings of creationists are not worthy of our time. However, the drivers of evolution are disputed, and undoubtedly will be refined by scientists in the future. Evolution occurred in steps, and the "survival of the fittest" driver does not appear to work well for all species. We should never abandon the sceptical method.

Nevertheless Pinker believes that the language instinct is one example of Darwinism not working well, as our brains guzzle energy, and he seems troubled as to why language is not hard-wired. Actually it seems to me that orthodox Darwinism can work quite well with language development. *Homo sapiens* is considered a generalist species, because it can adapt to a wide variety of environments. Generalist species have greater chances of survival because the inevitable changes in environment that occur in geological time destroy those species that exploit particular niches. However, man's "generalism" is based not on his body, which is clearly designed for a warm climate (it is tall, thin and hairless, and thus it releases heat easily). Like most Scots, I do not believe that my country and its climate are very suited to human habitation, but the inventiveness of past generations has rendered it quite acceptable and even occasionally pleasant. Man's adaptability is based entirely on his linguistic skills and the resulting ability to hand down technology from one generation to the next, and thus accumulate it. Pinker seems to forget that language is not just about communication (let alone pre-determined, hard-wired communication); it is also about memory. And not just personal memory but also the collective one. This combination is what I call the "social mind" (see Chapter Four). Complex methods of doing things can be handed down from one generation to another, and they can be altered either in accordance with technological progress or simply as adjustments to changes in environment, which would most frequently result from migration, including the relatively slow migration of farming communities. Even a very elaborate hard-wired language would simply have been incapable of providing this degree of adaptability. And this ability of ours to accumulate knowledge and technology to adapt to our environment is the sole basis for our exceptional generalism as a species

Pinker argues that we have a common language, which he calls "mentalese", and he seems to question whether language is essential to thought. We think in mentalese and then translate into language when we speak: "People do not think in English or Chinese or Apache; they think in the language of thought. This language of thought probably looks a bit like all these languages."[1] His argument is based on the fact that we often start writing a sentence and realise half way through that it is not what we wanted to say.[2] Absurd. Writing is a highly artificial activity, and we are creating something that is suspended in time. In speech and in our minds, we are always starting off on a sentence and then realising that it isn't going to work. We may start again, or more probably we will simply go back over part of it: "Look, I told you – didn't I – that we have to go to the cinema before we do the shopping – no, sorry, I mean the shopping before the cinema." This only proves that we often do things carelessly. I am willing to concede that if a fire were to break out in my house, I would not sit at my desk and laboriously say to myself, "A fire has broken out in the house and I should probably make my way to the door." Panic would take over and I would rush for the door. My heart would beat harder and my senses would become incredibly alert (something to which they are not very accustomed). My reactions and mental activity might not differ that much from any other animal. Equally if someone threw me a ball, I would process its trajectory in my mind and catch it, without using any language in my brain. Whether these quite complex mental processes can be defined as thought is arguable and obviously depends on what you consider thought to be. Let me turn the argument around: the ideas I have expounded on this or any other page – whether they are correct or not – could not have been thought through without language. And here is a more complex question: if I had thought them in a language other than English, would they have been exactly the same?

---

1. Steven Pinker, *The Language Instinct* (London: Penguin, 1995), p. 81.
2. *The Language Instinct* ..., p. 57.

As I asserted in the introduction, anyone who has translated large quantities of text from one language to another must know that translation is a process of approximation (this can easily be demonstrated by comparing various translations of the same book). The problems occur on several levels: as the phonology is different, it is impossible to recreate exactly the tone, the rhyme, the assonances, the puns; as the syntax is different, it may not be possible to organise the arguments in the same sequence, and it might be necessary to divide up sentences or bring them together; as the vocabulary is different, words will have entirely different semantic fields which will overlap in different directions, and even in the case of two Western European languages which share a common history dominated by Latin, there will be words that simply don't exist in the second language. And then the aesthetics of thought changes from one language to another: so an idea can occasionally be impossible to express in another language without making it appear laughable, pretentious, puerile or crass. This is not a question of bad translation, but of the limitations of translation. The fact that most of our more banal linguistic operations can be translated without difficulty must not divert our attention from the very restricted area where translation becomes awkward, because this area is precisely the one in which the most interesting things occur.

An experiment I read about some years ago provides a very different approach from Pinker's. The researchers had three cards: one had a picture of a man (A) kicking a ball, another a picture of the same man (A) about to kick a ball and another a picture of a different man (B) kicking a ball. A group of English-speakers and a group of Indonesian-speakers were asked to pair off two of the pictures. Most of the English-speakers paired off the two different men (A and B) both kicking the ball, and most of the Indonesians paired of the same man (A) kicking the ball and about to kick the ball. These extraordinary results would appear to reflect the different tense usage in the two languages. English has a clearly defined tense usage,[3] and generally Indonesian does not use tense, although it does have some marker words that are very occasionally used. Thus the expressions "he'll go", "he's going" and "he went" will follow the simplified pattern of "he go". As language (both vocabulary and grammar) is all about categorisation, the manner in which a language categorises the world could surely affect the manner in which a speaker categorises the world. This is one of the fundamental ways in which language governs the way we think, although language almost certainly affects our thought in more complex ways, particularly in the area where language comes closer to wider cultural questions, such as the structure of argumentation.

Our researchers formed a third group of bilingual English and Indonesian speakers, and the result was a mixture.[4] They probably had a great deal of difficulty coming to their decision, and interestingly bilingualism, the condition of three-quarters of the human population, is conspicuously ignored in Pinker's book. Moreover further tests showed that bilinguals behaved differently according to whether they were interviewed in English or Indonesian. This result was even more significant.[5]

Benjamin Lee Whorf, who was a leading proponent of the thesis that language affects the way we think, claimed

---

3. English tense use is more defined than, say, French, whose *past historique* tense has disappeared from the spoken language, but less defined than Kivunjo, the African language I referred to on p. 17.
4. "Babel's Children", *The Economist*, 8 January 2004. The researcher David Gil appears to have wanted to go further and question Chomskian theory as well, using the case of Riau Indonesian. Obviously I am not qualified to comment, but I am sceptical. The extremes overstate their case.
5. "Event representation: influence of aspect on thought", *Cognitive Science 1*, 8 July 2005, Zhenya-Anti (slides by Lera Boroditsky).

that Hopi does not have tense, while Pinker asserts that the anthropologist Ekkehart Malotki has proven that this is not the case. This leaves the rest of us in a little difficulty because, short of rushing off to do our own field studies, we cannot really decide (and besides, the time has probably come to leave the poor Hopi in peace). Things are not made any easier by the fact that Pinker dismisses the main counter-thesis to his own in a few pages of highly selective and rather crass arguments, whereas Whorf himself indulges in some highly abstract arguments full of jargon that occasionally makes your head spin, such as, "I shall say nothing in this paper of the nine voices (intransitive, transitive, reflexive, passive, semipassive, resultative, extended passive, possessive, and cessative); and of the nine aspects (punctual, durative, segmentative, punctual-segmentative, inceptive, progressional, spatial, projective, and continuative) I shall deal with only two."[6] Pinker – perhaps betraying a lack of better arguments – damns Whorf's theory for its apparent "perennial appeal … to undergraduate sensibilities", which of course means precisely nothing. Pinker may be right that Whorf was an unreliable researcher and even that Whorf takes his argument too far (much as Pinker does in the opposite direction), but Whorf's arguments are certainly worthy of serious examination and should not be flung aside as though unworthy of serious debate. His central argument is more or less summarised in the following passage:

> These [mystical and psychological] abstrac-
> tions are definitely given either explicitly in words

6. B.L. Whorf, *Language, Thought and Reality* (Cambridge Massachusetts: M.I.T. Press, 1973 (1956)), p.51. It is clear from this quote that the argument was substantially about what is a tense and what is a voice or "aspect". Intuitively it does seem very unlikely that any human society could have no concept of time, however rudimentary.

– psychological or metaphysical terms – in the Hopi language, or, even more, are implicit in the very structure and grammar of that language, as well as being observable in Hopi culture and behaviour.[7]

Curiously, the often valid argument used by Pinker against Whorf – that Whorf worked on translations of Apache for one of his studies, rather than through an intimate knowledge of the language – is equally true of the example Pinker takes from Malotki.[8] Pinker provides a very short sentence translated by Malotki, and asks us (who surely have less knowledge than poor Whorf) to take it as proof. Malotki's translation may be very good and his knowledge of the language better than Whorf's, but ultimately he is a linguist struggling with a less-known language, which is not his native tongue, and analysing it from the outside, while the most important distinctions he has to record are the nuanced ones non-native speakers often miss. In any event, this problem of translation and creating an exact parallel between two languages must militate against Pinker's ideas. When it comes to examining language diversity, we are always obliged to express ourselves through the constrictions of one particular language. While Pinker clings fast to the viewpoint of his own culture, it may well be that Whorf overcompensates in his desperate desire to understand the "other", a worthy aim but one that is also full of pitfalls.

Pinker confuses sameness and equality (and we are lucky in English that we have separate words for these two concepts). He is desperate to prove that underneath some trivial differences we are to all intents and purposes identical. He enthuses, "The anthropologists Brent Berlin and Scott Atran have studied folk taxonomies of flora and fauna. They have

---

7. *Language, Thought and Reality*, ... p. 59.
8. S. Pinker, *The Language Instinct*, ... p. 63.

found that, universally, people group local plants and animals into kinds that correspond to the *genus* level in the Linnaean classification system of professional biology."[9] This is indeed an unlikely claim, but it is the use of the word "universally" that tears away the veil of apparent academic objectivity. Are we to believe that these two intrepid academics studied flora and fauna in every one of the six thousand languages that still cling to life on our planet? They must have had prodigious linguistic abilities. But Pinker has not only discovered the universal language; he and his fellow psycholinguists have also discovered the "Universalized People". We are surely now well within the realm of pseudo-science.

Pinker robustly rejects the idea that his arguments are racist, and he is absolutely right. He points out that genetic differences between two randomly selected individuals within an "ethnic" group can be much greater than the ones between two different "ethnic" groups. Or as I would put it, every city, town or village has its thief, its megalomaniac, its poet, its dreamer, its athlete, its Don Giovanni, its gossip, etc. However, this equality of differences is always mediated through a language and a culture that are often very, very different. One almost gets the feeling that Pinker would have preferred language to be entirely hard-wired, and he is obviously convinced that the most significant part of it is. Although we can agree that the "language instinct" or instinct to learn is always the same, the thing that it absorbs into itself (the specific language or languages a child is exposed to) is not. Otherwise, there would be no point in there being variable language which, as Pinker himself makes clear, has a high cost in brain power and energy. It would be like giving autonomy to a region and being surprised when it makes different laws.

Language is often compared to a biological entity.

---

9. *The Language Instinct*, … pp. 442-3.

Although this is a useful analogy, the two differ in some very important respects: language is intangible and does not have any set life-span. By intangible, I mean that it has no matter and it has no place. Some people might object that it is material in that it exists in the neurons of the brains of every speaker, but clearly several counter-arguments immediately come to mind: no speaker has complete command even of his or her native tongue; every speaker has a different language according to class, dialect and ultimately idiolect (the language that reflects his or her own particular character and linguistic history); language is an idea with which every speaker is familiar, but which even the most expert grammarians and lexicographers cannot define with absolute precision; language carries the weight of history in its DNA; language is not only the sum of the actual words and sentences that have been thought or uttered – it is also a system for generating the infinity of possible sequences of words and sentences. It is true that a partial version of a language exists in the brains of every speaker, and that a language feeds off those partial versions (and indeed cannot survive without them, at least as an oral language), but that is not the language itself, which is an idea or, more prosaically, an agreed convention.

It can therefore be argued that every language exists to some extent outside humanity. It is rather like a Platonic idea in this sense: it is intangible and has a powerful influence over our being, and we are never quite capable of living up to it. I will examine this argument more fully in the next chapter, which is on the social mind. A human language is produced by humans and handed down in constantly changing forms from one generation to another. It is an individual being with a degree of autonomy, but it lives and breeds in a culture and society. It needs that culture and society to exist, and if that society starts to shrink, it eventually suffocates.

Language is also the product of military, political and economic happenstance, as well as the natural evolution of language involving such phonological phenomena as consonantal eclipse, final devoicing, etc. It is not even a clearly defined entity. Before the invention of national languages (before printing and often for some time after), continuums often made it impossible to determine where one language ended and another started. No language contains or could contain the sum of human knowledge and experience. Every language influences and is influenced by other aspects of culture, and as languages can straddle such cultural realities as religion and politics, there is scope for infinite gradations.

I do not wish to dismiss Pinker's book, which has its merits, particularly when it examines modern English. This Anglocentric work, which relies too much on argument by analogy (when overused this tends to imply a certain didactic contempt for the reader or, even worse, that the writer actually believes that analogy constitutes a proof), could only have been written in English and is therefore evidence against its own thesis. Pinker's humour is often successful but it does tend to confirm the French assertion in the film *Ridicule* "that the English don't do gentle wit (*esprit*)."[10] His linear method of argument is extremely Anglo-Saxon, and doesn't lack leaps in the logical sequence (non-sequiturs, which can of course be found in all languages, although Anglo-Saxon cultures are often remarkably tolerant of them). His chapter, "The Language Mavens", is full of very sensible criticisms of language pundits, but he doesn't realise that he is a bit of one himself (aren't we all?). He counters with his own rule – "the most important maxim of good prose: Omit needless words". Is this a universal linguistic truth, or is it just a dictate of American and English schoolteachers reflecting a fashion in post-Victorian English? After

---

10. *Ridicule*, directed by Patrice Leconte in 1996.

all, this dictate would banish one of my favourite writers, Henry Fielding, and most probably Dickens too. What appears neatly succinct to an Englishman or an American might appear abrupt and a little niggardly to an Italian or an Indian, while what might appear amusing and erudite to an Italian or an Indian might sound waffly and evasive to an Englishman or an American. His rule begs the question: what is a "needless word"?

I want to digress here not so much for an analogy as for an exploration of a parallel aspect of the human psyche. Freud was a very interesting speculative thinker and it is a pity that in accordance with positivist fashion, he chose to claim that his theories were scientific.[11] The hypothesis he proposed of an ego (self or rational self), an id (instinctive drives) and a super-ego (the dominant morality and social conventions picked up from the family and other institutions), is a valid refinement of previous philosophical models (whether it is actually correct, we are probably not yet in a position to say, but it certainly seems convincing enough to justify further speculations). Jonathan Haidt amusingly exploits a Platonic image to present Freud's model in the following manner: it is like a charioteer (the ego) driving a chariot (life) when the horse (the id) has bolted and his father (the super-ego) is telling him where he has gone wrong.[12] Here I am interested in the super-ego, which appears to have been universally deplored, even by Freud himself, as the cause of our anxieties and reason why, as Larkin put it, our parents fuck us up. It is seen as domineering and something

---

11. Poor Darwin was unintentionally responsible for much of this: his scientific ideas were so revolutionary and so influential that others naturally wanted to follow, even into fields where human knowledge was not yet ready for scientific exploration

12. Jonathan Haidt, *The Happiness Hypothesis* (London: Heinemann, 2006), p.3.

against which it is impossible to rebel. But surely if there is an instinctive facility within the human brain to internalise the accumulated moral and conceptual knowledge of a particular society, then it is probably good for that facility to be used.

The attitudes of parents to the super-ego and language in the twentieth century have increasingly come to resemble our attitude towards a new notebook (perhaps one of those leather-bound ones that are now provided in our consumer society). The empty notebook looks so clean and full of potential. Anything, literally anything, could be written there, but does the owner of the notebook feel that he or she possesses words worthy of so elegant a notebook? The notebook becomes both a threat and a promise: its very existence upbraids the owner for his inability to act, but its potential both excites and alarms. So it is with our children: now we are more aware of what we are doing – namely scribbling our stuff over their nice clean super-egos and their language usage – we are terrified of what we could do and overawed by the responsibility. We decide that we shouldn't impose our religious views (unless, of course, we are part of the swelling ranks of fundamentalists), we should not be too heavy about morality (inability to socialise and display oneself is now a greater crime than lying and stealing, and in extreme cases even violence), we do not choose their activities (as this would interfere with their freedom of choice, something they apparently must learn in order to perform in the free market), and of course Anglophone children are not given spelling tests, in spite of the fact that our bizarre spelling system necessitates this tiresome task. It is almost as though education (in the widest sense of the term, and not just learning in school) does not matter because the child's internal resources can cope and everything will somehow come right around the time of puberty.[13] Pinker's view of language fits into this cultural template: language is much more hard-wired than Chomsky suggested and those inner resources will produce the required result with a minimum of input from the adult world (paradoxically these attitudes are often accompanied by an adult intrusiveness in children's play, so that children have few opportunities to explore the world and discover things for themselves).

What if we got this all wrong, and instead of protecting the child by writing nothing, we should in fact have written much more than we did previously? If, instead of not telling our children about religion for fear of its undoubted divisiveness, we had told them about Christianity, Islam, Judaism, secularism and atheism, they might have ended up as believers in any one of them but they would surely be more tolerant of the others. Although there will always be fanatics, a more varied and complex moral education of this kind would produce in most cases a more profound knowledge of moral, ontological and theological argument, as well as a greater degree of scepticism (an extreme relativist might argue that I am merely expressing my own prejudice, because as a sceptic I am supposedly keen to propagate scepticism).

Of course Pinker might agree with some of my arguments and he does argue against the Standard Social Science Model, precisely because it interprets the human mind as a "blank slate".[14] Here the argument becomes complex: he rightly argues that we should not force reality to conform to our moral strictures, and should not therefore consider "biological determinism" to be inherently repugnant. Of course, scientific investigation should be wholly detached, but the point surely is that our biology predisposes us to a

---

13. Of course, this is something of a caricature, and this curmudgeonly tirade can only indicate a partial truth – a gross generalisation.
14. S. Pinker, *The Language Instinct*, … p. 427.

process by which we learn a unique culture. This system is a delicate balance of conservatism (led by the now infamous super-ego) and flexibility (led by language and rationalism). Over centuries and millennia this can lead to some very diverse societies and very diverse cultures. Margaret Mead might well have been hoodwinked, but this cannot be proof of what history of even just the last few centuries clearly demonstrates: not only societies but even generations think and act in markedly different ways.

By denying fundamental differences between languages and their influence on the way we perceive the world, Pinker is suggesting that change of language makes no difference. In his very brief comment on the galloping pace of language death, he does define this problem as "sad and urgent", and he does recall Krauss's often quoted and, I believe, entirely justified assertion that the electronic media are a form of "cultural nerve gas". However, the reader, particularly one who has given any consideration to the matter, is wholly underwhelmed. He does not even devote two pages to one of the most important subjects facing humanity in the field of sociolinguistics. You get the impression that what he defines as "Babel in reverse" is something we shouldn't be too concerned about. We might lose a few curious oddities, but human language will be able to survive. Be that as it may, his theory is important to us here because to deny that there is a significant distinction between languages is to devalue the importance of language difference and ultimately the need for it at all.

Pinker's arguments smack of current American thinking in many fields, and they all lead towards homogenisation. Americans do not fear homogenisation, as they believe that this process will always evolve around themselves, but their confidence is possibly misplaced. There is a culture of empire that is spreading through the English-speaking countries: this is damaging for the world and damaging for those countries. Homogenisation always appears superficially attractive. If we all speak the same language, think in similar ways, and have similar values and ambitions, then this will surely facilitate international trade, remove a whole series of unnecessary costs and, most importantly, decrease conflict between peoples. There is however no evidence that a common language lowers the likelihood of strife; indeed it may exacerbate it. Moreover, language diversity is essential for all languages, including the most powerful ones.

As with other aspects of our children's education, we should be teaching them more languages and doing more to maintain the diversity created by history and migration. A child with three languages will view the world in three different ways, and will have less fear or contempt of difference. We have to pass on our languages to our children, and because we now have many centuries of literature behind us, we can pass on the language of the past so that they can better understand the language of the present. If they have that greater knowledge of the specificity and indeed the restrictions of their own language (rather than perceiving it as an independent universe), they will be better able to express themselves.

Of course, language is not the only area in which we should be doing more to stimulate our children. In Hungary there has been a long tradition of attributing great importance to music in education, and it may be that this has produced good results in mathematics and science. The composer and expert on Hungarian folk music, Zoltán Kodály, claimed that music is an irreplaceable "intellectual food" and that "only art of intrinsic value is suitable for children."[15] As he died in

---

15. See the website of the Zoltán Kodály Pedagogical Institute of Music at www. kodaly-inst.hu/kodaly/balszoveg1.htm#3.

1967, he happily did not witness the global commercialisation of music, and his voice comes from a time when progress, which may no longer be sustainable as a concept, was at least based on values. He clearly believed that we have to intervene forcefully in our children's education, and I would argue what he may well have taken for granted: we have to demand more of our children, and they will have no difficulty in responding.

Kodály also implies that we should be choosy about the stimuli to which we expose our children, although he also emphasised the importance of allowing children to improvise. In spite of the liberal instincts of our generation, I believe that we have to revive this idea of carefully monitoring the language and music to which we expose our children. We need to impose some values on our children, as long as we are not too dogmatic, and this will give them the freedom and, most importantly, the tools to reject or modify those values. This is the task of each generation. If children are given too much freedom, they risk growing up without the ability to enjoy the intellectual pleasures of this life. Those who believe in laissez-faire will argue that that is their choice, but they're wrong; it was their parents' choice. Freedom too early produces young adults who are dependent on their parents materially and, what is worse, intellectually. In other words, by failing to give our children positive guidance, we deny them a real chance to rebel against us.

Language makes us what we are in essence, but the history of technology has burdened us for millennia with work, and now most recently with a leisure we don't know how to exploit intelligently. Language, the language of the garrulous and not the language of the passive consumer, is the way back to our human roots. Language and the exercise of language changes and develops the individual, triggers Cartesian existence, removes consciousness to some extent from physicality and places it in the intangible world of ideas. Like a musical instrument, it can only be played well by those who play it often.

Chapter Four

The creation of the social mind

"Promise me this," he said,
"Stay not the onward movement of your mind
And hold your course when barren talk
Pervades, and has no scope or sense
That drives and makes unconscious conscious thought"

He stood, and waving wide the circle of his hand,
he lifted up his spear. "The huddled dwellings on the hill
are not a home to change; and when the fighters fall upon the
plain,
the dullards shudder in their beds and weep their fears, as though
the gods could care
a damn about the frightened witless fools who fail to flee
the wrathful ruthless horde – the company of the strong."

"I have no quarrel with the settled folk," I said.
"Nor I," without a strain he stretched his arm
and pointed spear, its shining head, towards the tidy shacks,
"they are the mass, the herd, the herded demos whom we mock,
they built that fence to keep us out, and considered it an act of
will,"
he laughed , "but all they did was build a pen and turn them
selves to sheep.
For it is right that man should walk or ride upon the mountain ridge,
and carry spear and thrust it deep to make himself a man indeed."

"Who fashioned you that glinting spike of death?" I asked and
waited for the rift.
"A man whose skill is just our stock – to be culled and killed as
we would wish,
and if we are wise, we always leave some living to keep extant the
breed of forge-hands,
and sowers of seed that flocks the plain, and all the rest of settled,
soulless men,"
the sinewed sage, vigoured by his years, drew in his breath and
raised his spear
above his head, half threat – half gesture of his will to power.

"A force," I said, "whose only justification is its force, and has no
pleasure
but its exercise cannot be good, and good is when the soul divests
itself of power,
accepts its moral equalness." "Ha!" he cried, and joyous danced
around the spear
he'd skewered to the ground, "the vapid niceness of this man! But
what of life,
and nature too! Does the lion lick the lamb's wounds or bite?
Does it run
or aimless sit and make a meal of a meal after having
mealy-mouthed
mouthed a prayer to God? It has no god and nor should we."

"I heard the clamour of your words in little Europe's agora, and
felt
the textured smoothness and the heavy lightness of their weave,
their troubled truths, alluring lies, and clever, clever talk. You do
speak true when speaking of the little things, but not the big:
who are the strong who, unlike you, must travel in a pack?
And like a flood, a plague, a horde of certitudes go cutting down
the lives of industry and industry itself. What do you gain?"

"What do they lose?" he laughed again, "if losing lets them start
                                                        once more
to build upon their knowledge of the things this world contains.
                                                      They scurry
with their social mind and their own minds are not their own.
                                                      They worry,
as retainers of the rich, they slave for us, the strong who know
                                                      the reason
for which we came into this world: good war which hallows any
                                                  cause, and more
was made from its courageous course than fretting with one's
                                              neighbour's fate.
The fools! They value love – its soporific state – and underrate
                                              the force of hate."
"This is hubris; this is intellect that holds high opinion of itself and
                                              structured ways
to be a man. It belongs to you but not to them, the company that
                                                          flays
the folk who work and love and hope in less engrandised
                                                  circumstance,"
I answered him with bitter rectitude. "For you would condemn
                                                          chance
to always favour bold and not reflective men unless they think
                                                    like you.
Your gayness is your rash redress of what your father never knew:
the power of pleasure and the pleasure of the power to take what
                                              pleasure wants
and should not have."

Down they came, the company of power, and what a motley crew:
one wore a helmet and one a tricorn hat, one dressed the admiral
                                              of the fleet,
another was a moghul lord and brandished yataghan, and yet can
                                                  these few

so much power bring to bear upon the sword-less folk? And how
well they knew
the artless and inflated art of being grand! Cold sneer, sadistic
laugh complete
with blackened teeth, a scar, a stare of maddened haughty ice that
can browbeat
the trodden folk. And these alone mark out these grander men
whose greatness
draws on their disdainful look and looks not at the plainness of
their fateless,
surly self that lives in the now and builds our hell on earth:
removes our plenty and leaves a land of dearth.

"Here are my brothers," the wise man sang, and grinned in
Dionysian glee,
"I have lauded all your lordly deeds and more, and asked no fee,"
he servile nodded to their bloated selves, "except your pleasure."
He kissed the chief man's hand: "Your victories are my treasure!"
"You're right," the potentate pronounced while swinging high his
scimitar to catch pure light,
to form the figure of the strong, to carve his name on centuries long
with epic deeds of those who kill not for vengeance but for thrill
of wilful strength that idles – erratic and fanatic, unreasoned
and unseasoned by the conscious; thus inhuman in its fatal,
fateful will to be
the thing that is and cannot see the weakness of the wilful state
that hears no plea
of compassion

And down it came and severed air and rived the wise man's head
of hair.
"Goodbye, old man, you served us well; I speed you on the road
to hell
so you can Dionysian dance the well-marked way your

well-intended stance
marked out when spinning your words to serve us killers of
contempted herds.
His father was a priest, a dogmat of the Christian cult who
straight-backed walked
amongst the herd and joyless confirmed them in their herdish
ways and talked
the talk of life to come and hopes eternal beyond the fierceness of
our rule.
He stole their bodies and he stole their souls; the coarseness of his
school
left little hope of living life up to its brim and going beyond the
petty part the pawn
plays in my hands," the chief man roared, while wiping blood
from the blade he'd drawn
light-heartedly. "But what of him, the son who came from those
he loved to scorn?"
"He served us well with all his intellectual force and traitored
those who work upon the hill.
And set off on his ineffectual course to go beyond while doing ill
to those for whom he should have cared. As one of us he could
not be:
we do no thinking in our bold equestrian crowd.
Proudly we get others to do that paltry thing,
as others do our digging, forests cut
and fill our coffers with their well-gotten gains:
do they not see how we can govern
and leave so little for their enduring pains?"

I wept and kept my invisible distance from their jocund and
unruffled wrath;
I buried genius in the sands after placing the spear in both hands;
I prayed to God for the godless seer and longed for a time when
he could appear

harmless for his bold falsehoods. Dust denoted the diminution of
the brutal behemoth
That he so loved.
Zarathustra's Last Interview[1]

Language is part of an enormous apparatus, once wholly
intangible but now increasingly tangible, that every human
society possesses, and this apparatus could not exist without
language – or rather a language that is equally intangible and
not hard-wired. Apart from language, this apparatus contains technology, literature (either oral or written), religious
and philosophical systems, behavioural patterns (etiquette
– that quaint word), and all other forms of knowledge that
hold a society together and make it work. This apparatus
I have decided to call the "social mind".[2] Language is the
stone or endocarp of the social mind, and all the other cultural emanations the pulp or mesocarp: every part is inter-
related in a healthy fruit, but the stone is distinct and more
durable. Language can and does survive into entirely different cultural contexts.

Like language, the boundaries between social minds are
not at all clear. Geographically, where does one end, and
another start? Even in this age of nation states, boundaries
do not follow linguistic borders and communities coexist.
Then there is the question of mass bilingualism and
bi-culturalism. As the centuries pass and inevitable changes
come about, at what point do you say that one social mind
has died and another has been born? When examining
tangible culture, this is all very clear: a castle is there once
it has been built and it is no longer there once it has fallen

1. This poem also appeared in my collection of poetry, *Presbyopia* (Sulaisiadar:
Vagabond Voices, 2009), pp. 35-40.
2. I first coined this term in my second novel, *The Berlusconi Bonus* (Edinburgh:
Luath Press, 2005), p. 78.

down, but the intangible of a method of building a castle or fortification does not always have such a clearly defined start and finish. This is the problem of periodisation in history, which generally reflects the issues that historians consider to be most important within their own generations, although occasionally events occur that are so catastrophic that no one can challenge them.

Like language, the social mind is never the possession of any single individual, however learned. And because so much of it is intangible and constantly shifting, it too should be considered an idea or form, not exactly in the Platonic sense, as here I use the term "idea" or "form" as a fluid and, what is more, a dependent phenomenon – dependent on the reality Plato considered merely shadows. Thus it is now a contingent, unrealisable perfection, rather than an eternal one. It is most definitely there, we feel we know what it is, but we cannot define it or ascertain its exact contours and borders. Perhaps it would be better to define the concept of the social mind as a kind of inverted Platonism. The creation of ideas occurs within the social mind, and that is the core distinction. According to the concept of the social mind, a society creates the idea organically through the sum of its individuals and the power relations between them, while in Platonism the idea is a detached and permanent reality that acts on our own shadowy world. For the concept of the social mind, every society has its unattainable ideals that affect its behaviour and tell an outsider a great deal about the nature of that society. There is an ideal table (always supposing the society in question uses tables), there is an ideal male and female physical beauty, there is an ideal language, there is an ideal education and, most sublime of all, there is an ideal republic, to which people are willing to devote and even sacrifice their lives. I am not an absolute relativist, although I freely admit that these ideals are at best partial truths and, in any event, entirely contingent (as are so many wonderful things). Nor am I saying that there is no absolute and eternal truth behind these ideals, although I and, I suspect, everyone else have no way of knowing what that absolute and eternal truth could be, or indeed if there is one.

Here we are interested in how the social mind influences language and how language, which is part of the social mind, influences the rest of the social mind. In pre-literate societies or societies in which the literary or the liturgical language is not normally spoken even by the ruling class, language is very fluid and reflects changing power relations as well as the rest of the rules of generational shift in language; it is a constant organic evolution that goes pretty much unrecorded. In literate societies and particularly post-printing ones, the layers of ideas and linguistic forms become almost infinite, because so much survives. For instance, the ideal of Saint Augustine's *City of God* is an alien concept to modern humanity, and yet it is not irrelevant, if for no other reason than that it continues to be read, albeit mainly in translation. Because it and so many other works have exercised such enormous influence and still do to some small extent, our daily speech still contains the presence of Latin, the language it was written in, which can only now be properly called "dead" for the first time since its birth two and a half millennia ago.

The social mind is of relevance to this book, because the technological changes that have occurred in the way we communicate through language have also caused enormous changes in the nature of the social mind. The modern social mind is perhaps not so much a social mind as a compendium of social minds or indeed the Universal Social Mind or the Global Mind. I will attempt to examine the twin evolution of language and the social mind, because they cannot be separated. The social mind contrasts with the individual mind, which is the sum of knowledge contained within any particular individual from any particular cultural and linguistic community.

A hunter-gatherer society would initially appear to have a very limited social mind, as it has no property, its technology is limited and its food is provided by nature. But as this was the generation of humanity that generated language (albeit in a manner that is not at all clear to us), language was something they needed and in all probability it was a means to store knowledge. Hunter-gatherer societies were numerically small and covered vast territories with varied fauna and flora. They needed to have an excellent science of these things, which recorded what was edible, how it could be eaten, at what times it was available, and what was dangerous and how it could be avoided. They also needed accurate geographical knowledge. We know from Francis Yates (talking, of course, about a much later stage in human development) that the human mind finds it easier to remember language (or what we might call "oral text") when it can associate it with a series of images along an itinerary. It may be that in the hunter-gatherer society, the process was reversed: the text indicated the route; the text was the roadmap. The familiar text was used to recall the itinerary rather than the familiar itinerary to recall the text. This is certainly what appears to be suggested by the "songline" in Australian aboriginal society. It is doubtful that we can entirely base our understanding of the original hunter-gatherer society on modern hunter-gatherer societies, because the latter all survive in a state of near extinction, driven to the margins of their original territories and forced to cohabit with modern consumer society, usually in some quite dependent way. However, these beleaguered communities can provide us with a vague understanding of their past, although there is still the almost impossible task of reconstructing what has already been lost.

Galileo also made Yates's point in his *Sidereus Nuncius* (1610): "Such is the condition of the human mind that every memory fades if not stimulated by images from the external world that continuously manifest themselves to it."[3] The inner world of the memory and the outer world perceived by the senses are inextricably linked together. Perhaps the most stunning illustration of this reality is the following Hasidic story:

> In order to honour God, my grandfather's father left his home very early, at the first light of day. He went into the wood and followed a path that only he had knowledge of, until he came to this meadow at the foot of a hill. On approaching a spring, he stood before an oak tree and recited an ancient, sublime and secret prayer in Hebrew.
>
> His son, my father's father, also left his home quite early, and went into the wood along the path his father had shown to him. And yet he did not go as far, because he was short of breath and had so many troubles weighing on his mind. He had found a birch tree near a burn, and it was in front of that tree that he would intone the Hebrew prayer that he had learnt by heart as a child. Thus, he too was able to honour God.
>
> His elder son, my father, had little memory, was less pious and did not enjoy robust good health. Hence he did not get up so early, and only went to one of his gardens near his house, where he had planted a sapling, and in order to honour God he mumbled a

---

3. Galileo, *Sidereus Nuncius*, 1610. The quote appears in the first paragraph of the book and the dedication to Grand Duke Cosimo II.

few Hebrew words in a very inaccurate manner and often full of mistakes.

And as for me, I have neither memory nor time; I have forgotten where the wood is, know nothing about burns and springs, and am unable to recite a single prayer. However, I get up early and tell this story: this is the manner in which I honour God.[4]

This story has many meanings, and perhaps we can all infer new ones. For me, the most remarkable element is the manner in which the decaying memory is accompanied by a shortened itinerary. This cultural atrophy is also reflected in the decreasing nobility of the external world whose stimuli Galileo tells us are the key to memory. First there is the oak visited by the great-grandfather, then the birch discovered by the grandfather, then a mere sapling whose genus is not specified, and finally no tree at all for the seemingly negligent narrator, whose self-awareness perhaps saves him before his God. This process of generational decay is another theme in this book, and is caused by technology which brings, however, its own compensations by unlocking access to so much readily available knowledge. The story also narrates our retreat from nature and our losing battle with time. We modern people may well admire the great-grandfather, but we probably have more sympathy for the great-grandson who narrates. He is one of us.

Very speculatively, one could argue that hunter-gatherer societies stored an enormous amount of information in poetry and songs and would therefore have had languages designed for the production of oral text in verse. Consider

---

4. This story appears in Carlo Severi, *Il percorso e la voce* (Turin: Einaudi, 2004), p. 3, who in turn took it from É. Wiesel, *Célébration Hassidique* (Paris: Éd du Seuil, 1972).

for a moment the syntax of Zulu, clearly not the language of a hunter-gatherer people, but of a farming one with a highly evolved and militarised state. I chose the example simply because it still contains syntactical elements that create endless alliterations that versify everyday language. In the sentence, "our handsome country appears, we love it", the subject "country" dominates the sentence by affecting all the other words in the sentence with non-functional inflections. The result is something extremely elegant, although the sentences were chosen for comparative purposes and are sometimes rather unlikely (the inflections are italicised):

ilizwe	letu	elichle	liyabonakala silitanda	
(country)	(our)	(handsome)	(appears)	(we love)
isizwe	setu	esichle	siyabonakala sisitanda	
(nation)	(our)	(handsome)	(appears)	(we love)
izizwe	zetu	ezichle	ziyabonakala sizitanda	
(nations)	(our)	(handsome)	(appears)	(we love)
izintombi	zetu	ezinchle	ziyabonakala sizitanda	
(girls)	(our)	(handsome)	(appears)	(we love)

As we are talking about human language, it will come as no surprise that this is not always so regular. "m" and "n", in particular, appear to trigger a more complex pattern of assonance.

amazwe	etu	amachle	ayabonakala	siwatanda
(countries)	(our)	(handsome)	(appears)	(we love)
umuntu	wetu	omuchle	uyabonakala	simtanda
(man)	(our)	(handsome)	(appears)	(we love)
intombi	yetu	enchle	iyabonakala	siyitanda
(girl)	(our)	(handsome)	(appears)	(we love)[5]

5. Otto Jespersen, *Language: Its Nature, Development and Origin* (London: George Allen and Unwin, 1922), p.353.

The aesthetics of language is called rhetoric, and in modern Anglo-Saxon culture, rhetoric is considered an unalloyed evil – such is our utilitarian approach to language and much else besides. However, rhetoric is merely a systematic study of those forms, figures and sounds that, for reasons that are usually unclear, are pleasant to the human ear. In my education, at least (and I think it was pretty typical of the English-speaking world at the time), rhetoric was proscriptive, but never, of course, called rhetoric. So I was told not to repeat the same word in a sentence. Good advice, but I was never told that the repetition of the same root in a sentence while inflecting it in a different way is pleasing, as in Dante's *Cred'io ch'ei credette ch'io credesse* or Plautus's *Homo homini lupus* (polyptoton). Moreover, if a sound is repeated not once but twice, then it can have a powerful effect, and again Dante provides us with an excellent example at the gates of hell: *Per me si va nella città dolente, per me si va nell'eterno dolore, per me si va tra la perduta gente* (anaphora). The single repetition of a word or sound can be pleasing if the first use comes at the end of a clause or sentence, and the next one at the beginning of the following clause or sentence (anadiplosis), and even in the same sentence if there is an inversion of a related pair of words, as in "They do not eat to live, but live to eat" (chiasmus). Of course, the random application of rhetorical forms would have laughable results; they have to be used sparingly, and the question of rhetoric is not unrelated to the question of register (Chapter Six). However, knowledge of rhetoric is useful to writers and, in particular, to poets. The rhetoric we are, or rather used to be, familiar with in the West is Greek rhetoric, which displaced other European rhetorical systems, many of which had been part of oral traditions (such as alliterative poetry of Germanic languages). It would be interesting to see the results of a comparative study of rhetorical systems to assess the degree of overlap (suggesting a kind of "natural" or innate rhetoric).

Another apparently inherent aspect of human language is the persuasive power of the story, as opposed to reasoned argument. Consider, for example, the following story from the New Testament:

> And the scribes and Pharisees brought unto him a woman taken in adultery; and when they had set her in the midst, they say unto Him, Master, this woman was taken in adultery, in the very act. Now Moses in the law commanded us, that such should be stoned: but what sayest thou? This they said, tempting him, that they might have to accuse him. But Jesus stooped down, and with his finger wrote on the ground, as though he heard them not. So when they continued asking him, he lifted up himself, and said unto them, He that is without sin among you, let him first cast a stone at her. And again he stooped down, and wrote on the ground. And they which heard it, being convicted by their own conscience, went out one by one, beginning with the eldest, even unto the last; and Jesus was left alone, and the woman standing in the midst. When Jesus lifted up himself, and saw none but the woman, he said unto her, Woman, where are those thine accusers? hath no man condemned thee? She said, No man, Lord. And Jesus said unto her, Neither do I condemn thee: go, and sin no more.[6]

Religious teachers have always known that stories are more persuasive than reasoned argument. Reasoned argument

---

6. John 8. 3-11.

cannot be considered inherent to language, and therefore requires greater effort on the part of the listener or reader. Conversely, humans are exceptionally adept at interpreting the moral significance of stories (*exempla*). I will attempt to distil the significance of this episode into reasoned prose:

> Although there are a set of rules by which we should live and by which we should be punished, real morality is not concerned with the behaviour of others, but with the behaviour of the self. This obsession with individual responsibility to God and man, and the resulting humiliation of the self is the great innovation of Christianity.

The result is dull in comparison for two reasons. Firstly it lacks all narrative tension, and secondly, it loses all its nuances and ambiguities. The event was caused by the scribes' desire to trap Jesus. His immediate reaction was to ignore them and hope that they would go away. He clearly found both punishing the woman and releasing her to be less than perfect outcomes. First-century Galilee must have been a society divided over how to treat an adulteress, as otherwise the question would not have been perceived to be dangerous by both Jesus and the scribes. Moreover, the scribes were not quite as bad as they might first appear, because when challenged by Jesus in the manner he chose, they slunk away in shame "convicted by their own conscience" (which means, at least, that they had one). There are a lot of things the text does not tell us (this is another privilege of narrative): we do not know what he was writing on the ground and we do not know what his real attitude to adultery was. Even the central message could be argued over, if it were not for the fact that elsewhere Jesus explicitly states, "Judge not, and ye shall not be judged: condemn not, and ye shall not be condemned: forgive, and ye shall be forgiven."[7] Narrative is extremely potent, but it is also ambiguous; hence we have also developed reasoned argument, which is less spontaneous and more laboured. Hume and Kant do not sell as well as Austen and Dickens. To some extent, our civilisation with all its merits and all its faults (often horrendous crimes of which previous societies were incapable) has been built on reason endlessly defending itself from our innate irrationalism (power intersects this axis, as it exploits both the rational and the irrational).

I started to reflect on the persuasiveness of the stories we tell our children, when I read that Garibaldi suffered so many hardships because he wished to emulate the story of Cincinnatus. Needless to say, the historical accuracy of these stories is irrelevant to this argument. It is probably very important how such stories are glossed by the teacher when a child first hears it; the story of the possible stoning of the adulteress in the New Testament, which I have just quoted, had an enormous effect on me as a child, but the teacher set the framework by telling us that adultery, which was not explained, was not the sort of misconduct that deserved such a cruel punishment. Fifty or a hundred years earlier, a teacher might have presented the story in a different light. The story of Cincinnatus is the story of an honest and courageous man who accepts the position of dictator to save Rome from a crisis. Having successfully carried out this mission and served his term, Cincinnatus returned to his farm and ploughed his fields, while refusing all the financial benefits of power. It is possible that in the climate of nationalism, a new force in European politics engendered by the Napoleonic Wars, Garibaldi's teachers found the story of Cincinnatus particularly pertinent. Nice, his native city, had been annexed by France during the wars and for

---

7. Luke 6. 37.

the first seven years of his life. Clearly it was not just the story that so influenced Garibaldi, but the story and the moment. Cincinnatus may not have existed or, if he did, he may not have carried out such deeds, but Garibaldi most certainly did, and he consciously established the link by calling himself "Dictator" of Sicily and then Southern Italy, and by relinquishing power immediately to go and plough the stony fields of his farm on the Island of Caprera. When he left, he only took a few bags of coffee, to which he appears to have been addicted. Stories, lacking a precise meaning, constitute a store of ideas held in the social mind, and are used to maintain the delicate balance between continuity and flexibility so essential to the survival of human societies. Like language, their openness to reinterpretation is so great that they should perhaps be called a language of ideas rather than a store.

The power of stories remains, as do the problems that this causes. The ruin of Madame Bovary is that she takes a certain kind of literature too seriously. She believes that there is a reality reflected in those stories, while in fact they have no purpose other than to entertain and make publishers of romantic novelettes rich. Stories of the past were equally lacking in reality, but they served a purpose – the principal one being the glorification of warfare through heroes such as Achilles, Fionn and Loki. Stories, at their most effective, can express truths that escape rational argument (perhaps this is a definition of literature in its more restricted and exalted sense – or one to add to the many): Victor Serge's *The Case of Comrade Tulayev* says more about the complex realities of Soviet Russia in the thirties than any number of tiresome political tracts, and there certainly were a lot of tiresome tracts written on that subject. On the other hand, the rationalist instinctively distrusts stories because, like rhetoric, they are open to abuse. They can be used to seek the truth as in the case of Serge's novel, but they can also be used to distort it: they are the raw material of propaganda and harmful escapism. Rationalism may not be our natural state, but it has certain undoubted advantages. In any case, rationalism is here for very clear historical reasons; it is the result of a process, because at a certain stage in its development, the social mind takes on a life of its own and starts to govern the individual mind. The trigger for this increasing autonomy of the social mind has always been the technology of the word.

Early hunter-gatherers may, then, have had vast vocabularies, a great store of stories, poetry and songs (themselves a store of moral precepts and methods for interpreting the world), an accumulated knowledge of their environment through observation, and only a limited recourse to rational and systematic thinking. As the degree of specialisation would have been minimal, the distinction between the individual mind and the social mind would also have been minimal, or to put it another way, their individual mind may have been larger than our own, but their social mind must have been much smaller.

With the advent of farming communities and the organisation of increasingly large states to defend such communities from other states and from nomadic peoples, there was a greater need to keep records of property and to administrate the business of state. Given the urgency of that need, it is perhaps surprising that it took so long for writing to be invented.

Like all great inventions, writing did much more than resolve the demand that had led to its creation. Some time in the fourth millennium before Christ, the so-called cuneiform script was invented. The patterns of its wedge-shaped marks were used to denote both sounds and ideograms in a dozen languages of the Middle East, including Sumerian, Akkadian, Babylonian, Assyrian and Hittite. The writer used a clay tablet which in the early period was left to harden in the sun but later was fired in a kiln.

What interests us is how this changed language. Very quickly writing must have been used to record oral literature: most famously we have *Gilgamesh* (an Akkadian epic work found on 12 incomplete tablets) from the middle of the third millennium BC. It may be assumed that literary works went further back because extant material exists mainly due to a subsequent invention – that of the library. Initially archaeologists working for the British took little notice of the heap of broken crockery with patterned surfaces, when they broke into the King Ashurbanipal's library in Nineveh (Iraq). The oldest literature in the world had fallen with the wooden ceilings from the higher storeys, and crumbled under the feet of those who rushed to take vases, weapons and bronze and ivory ornaments – the incidentals of that seventy-one-room palace of learning.

By making possible written literature, cuneiform started the process whereby the spoken word lost its mnemonic significance, because there now existed a more efficient and reliable method for storing knowledge. Literature no longer evolved organically, but became something, dare I say it, dead. Someone who dared not only to say it, but also to shout it from the rooftops was Jean-Paul Sartre, with his talent for overstatement: "We all know that graveyards are peaceful places, and the most pleasant ones are called libraries."[8] Now Sartre is dead, and his books too are "written by a dead person about dead things", but as I like these particular graveyards, I continue to read and enjoy Sartre, even if he is temporarily out of fashion. But then Sartre's

---

8. Jean-Paul Sartre, *Che cos'è la letteratura?* (Milan: il Saggiatore, 1976), p. 66; original title: *Qu'est-ce-que la littérature?* (Paris: 1947).

major fault was that he was too much of his time, and he misses the point about the deadness of literature. For him, the problem was that the writer had to be engaged with his times, while critics exploited the dead writers to avoid the real issues. He was probably right about the critics, but he is wrong about the deadness of literature. Literature remains relevant, even powerful and, I believe, essential to the psychological health of our societies, but when it became written rather than oral, it became a set of unchanging trophies attached to a certain name, and until relatively recent times, a canon. Whereas oral literature constantly renews itself in the language of each generation, written literature remains embedded in the language of the past and starts to fade. Now that the human voice can be recorded, we can see that that process of fading is much more rapid with the spoken word, because it retains all its contingent features (accent, syntax, vocabulary, tone and social context). This is why British films of the thirties appear to come from such a distant past (possibly even for those who can remember the thirties), but the written word takes longer to appear strange and when it does so, it is often to its benefit (the survival of the King James Bible, in spite of many attempts to see it off with translations into "modern" English, is perhaps the best example of this). Nevertheless, text does fade, just as the colours of an old master fade, and we risk losing what is salvageable by deifying the writing of the past. And yet there can be no doubt about what we gain from the ability of writing to preserve the thoughts of past.

"Dead" is a polemical exaggeration, as the literature of dead writers continues to actively affect the way we think (perhaps less now than in the past). Established literature teaches but also upbraids. The luckiest writers were those who wrote when their literatures were young: Dante, Shakespeare, Luther, Pushkin. These men did not write in a language; they invented one. They had no great men of letters wagging their fingers at them: telling them not to split an infinitive or to avoid starting a sentence with a conjunction. They borrowed from different dialects and indeed languages. They didn't have to invent their own rhetoric, because this too could be borrowed, and their good fortune was that they had often imperfectly understood these other rhetorics. They didn't have to reinvent the wheel; they just had to decide what material to use in making one. Much to their credit, both Dante and Shakespeare were for centuries considered crude and uncultured writers.

The works of Homer are thought to have been composed around 2,000 BC and written down around 1,000 BC, and that would have been the time in which the version we have was frozen for all posterity. If they had been able to write at the time of composition, we would have a different version and very probably it would have been composed in a different manner by literate poets. The works supposedly composed by Homer are written literature that still reflects its oral origins. In oral society, poetry was both mnemonics and aesthetics; with the invention of writing the former receives the first of many blows: it does not disappear immediately, but slowly loses importance, while aesthetic discoveries became more difficult to lose and therefore continuously enriched each other. Poetry becomes more sophisticated, but the poet less skilled.

With the invention of writing and more particularly with the accumulation of written material stored in libraries, part of the social mind becomes tangible. It is no longer the case that everything that is not remembered must die without leaving any trace, and this changes the nature of language. Writing releases the human brain from the onerous task of remembering the most important things, and creates an entirely new kind of language: prose. Writing may also be the driver behind the gradual simplification of language mentioned in Chapter Three, particularly after the invention of printing. The complex ornamentation of language may no longer be required because of the withering of its mnemonic role. Personally I consider this thought a highly speculative one, as the more probable driver for simplification is imperialism, which expands use of a language to a vast number of new speakers over a relatively short period of time; this creates the need for less-inflected forms such as a shift from noun cases to prepositions.

With prose, human language starts its long journey towards rationalism. This is how Lucien Polastron describes Ashurbanipal's library in Nineveh:

> The patterned ceramic bisques of 1,200 different texts tell us what a royal library was like twenty-five centuries ago. To our eyes it was more primitive poetry than jurisprudence: invocations, ritual formulas, prophecies, Sumerian dictionaries, epic tales including *The Saga of Gilgamesh*, the creation story and the myth of Adapa the first man (all things that otherwise we would not have known), scientific handbooks and treatises, and popular tales such as *The Poor Man of Nippur*, precursors of *A Thousand and One Nights*. Following the demise of Ashurbanipal and his intellectual legacy, the sources after 631 BC go silent on this great enthusiast for books, his death and the ruin of his worldly estate.[9]

Personally I am struck by the range of genres gathered together in this early attempt to systemise and catalogue human knowledge.

---

9. Lucien Polastron, *Libri al rogo* (Milan: Edizioni Sylvestre Bonnard, 2006), p. 16-17 (original title: *Livres en feu*, Paris: Éditions Denoël, 2004).

The literate relate to their languages in a different way from the illiterate. The difference is similar to that of a car-driver who understands how a car works and a car-driver who doesn't. The literate know how a language works, because they have seen it broken up into its constituent parts: words, clauses and sentences. The artificiality of writing turns the literate into artificial speakers; they lose the spontaneity of their language use, and if they have read a great deal, then they become aware of how their language has evolved and is evolving. The ensuing loss of innocence can either stultify or liberate, but in any event, writing, like all the technological changes discussed in this chapter, brings a gain and a loss. It is up to the individual to make use of that gain and minimise that loss.

Writing obviously presupposes the existence of an author or indeed authors, but just as importantly it presupposes the existence of a reader. In no other art does the "end-user" play such an active part (and literature is the least artistic of the arts). All art takes full possession of the artist's mind, but writing has this same effect on the reader. This is not to imply that listeners to music or viewers of a painting do not have to use sensitivity and intelligence; it is just that reading entirely isolates the mind from the other senses, and demands that the imagination bypasses or rather substitutes for them. Books are such an efficient way of transferring information and sensations, and we are all so good at it, for the simple, powerful reason that language is what we do and what we are. It is no exaggeration to say that the *ideal* reader has to be as creative as the writer. On this point, Sartre cannot be bettered:

> Reading is therefore an act of generosity, and the writer requires of readers not the application of an abstract freedom, but the gift of all their beings, with

their passions, prejudices, sympathies, sexual tem-
peraments and sets of values.[10]

Reading is "an act of generosity", and readers are required
to recreate everything within their minds, particularly in narrative works. Reading is opening the door of one's mind to
other people – to the "other". No wonder then that reading
(paradoxically a very solitary act circumscribed by a particular language) must surely be considered the artistic activity
that most increases tolerance and openness to other people.
Ashurbanipal, our bibliophilic Assyrian monarch, always
chose native administrators for his various imperial possessions, and very possibly this enlightened approach hastened
the end of his empire and the learning that he had amassed.
In a sense, readers perform a literary work to themselves in
their brains. That performance can be of varied quality: the
reader might know the accents described and recreate them
in his or her brain, as well as tone, sentiment or register (this
is particularly difficult in English, because we don't have a
serviceable system for reproducing phonology on the page
– and so the reader has to work that bit harder). Complex
non-fiction works require the reader to ponder each argument carefully, and that often means the reader has to take
notes or gloss the text. Our hurried manner of consuming
things has been extended to reading, and this means that
the modern writer is supposed to adapt to a similarly frenetic
pace. Somebody in a hurry does not want too many obsta-
cles or too many demands. But good reading, like good writing, demands time and cannot compete with the television,
the playstation and perpetual motion. Reading is the key
to a rational knowledge of the world, because we can only
understand the world rationally through our use of language,
even though language does have its inherent limitations as

---

10. J.-P. Sartre, *Che cos'è la letteratura?* ..., p. 86.

a rational tool. The fact that reading doesn't feel like hard work is further proof that it is an activity appropriate to our natures.

It is difficult to assess the degree to which writing led to a professionalisation of the word and the invention of an intellectual elite. The principal features of an, albeit highly exclusive, literate world were present from a very early time: an obsession with reading and book-collecting, a weariness with the word and a surfeit of ideas. This was more than the powerful wanted, when they went looking for a tool to rationalise the administration of large territories. Writing took off and, although still very much an exclusive province, became menacing because of vastness of the information it accumulated.

Zhuangzi, who believed that excessive reading was likely to clog up the brain, wrote, "The spirit that persists in studying grows bigger every day; the spirit that pursues the Tao grows smaller every day. By growing smaller one achieves *wuwei* (non-action); nothing is impossible when one does not take action."[11] And Zhuangzi wrote at a time when writing was still a ponderous affair, often involving large bamboo rods. Francis Bacon believed that excessive reading had the opposite effect: "To spend too much time in studies is sloth; to use them too much for ornament is affectation; to make judgement wholly by their rules is the humour of the scholar. They perfect nature, and are perfected by experience."[12] There are two elements of interest here, one concerning Bacon's times and one his nation. The Renaissance, which arrived late in England, was the period in which texts were tested against "experience" and their authority was first challenged. But Bacon's pronouncements, although not original in that first

---

11. Quoted in Polastron, *Libri al rogo*, 2006, p. 89.
12. Francis Bacon, *Essays* (London: J.M. Dent & Sons, 1972), p. 150 (L).

sense, have a tone that is peculiarly English. They are an early example of the English anti-intellectualism expressed by a consummate intellectual, which was to become the mainstay of a very fruitful tradition for many centuries, before it degenerated into a mere excuse for intellectual disengagement. Interestingly Bacon adds, "Crafty men contemn studies; simple men admire them." Admiration for learning would have been widespread in England at the time, just as in the rest of Europe.

Whilst the Chinese Taoist thinker of the fourth century BC criticised excessive reading because it could engender activism, and the hyper-active Englishman of the late-sixteenth and early-seventeenth centuries criticised its potential detachment from the observation of the real world, Plato simply referred to Aristotle, perhaps a little sarcastically, as "the reader", and Aristotle's position as the patron saint of all pedants may have been due to the fact that, unlike his more brilliant teacher, he didn't know when to stop reading and let his own thoughts develop themselves.

No doubt the new intellectual elite itself felt overwhelmed by enormity of learning. Its members also probably felt underappreciated by the ignorant, stymied by the ambitious and not a little alienated by the solitude of their profession. The ivory tower had been built, and with it came the varying mix of hubris and generosity that typifies the intellectual. Writing may have invented the intellectual, but it was a god that immediately humiliated its creation, by demonstrating the intellectual's ignorance in relation to the great mass of human learning. By turning the social mind into something tangible, writing displayed learning in its physical bulk, which could be weighed, counted and quantified. Polastron informs us that the 30,000 ceramic bisques collected with shovels from the ruins of Mesopotamia between 1849 and 1854 occupied 100 cubic metres and were roughly equivalent to 500 of our 500-page quarto editions.

This, of course, was the weakness of the new media for recording language: its physicality meant that it could rot, crumble or burn in an accidental fire. It also meant that hostile forces could destroy the accumulated learning of centuries within a few hours (in this the cumbersome clay tablets actually had an advantage over the other media such as papyrus, parchment, vellum and paper, as fire did not destroy them but rather it vitrified them). The fear and loathing inspired by these great heaps of congealed garrulousness we call libraries is a matter of historical record, and Lucien Polastron decided to write his exhaustive work on the subject on seeing the destruction of Sarajevo Library in 1992.

I have tried to distinguish a pattern, but it is not at all easy. Julius Caesar accidentally caused the first destruction of the famous library in Alexandria, and coming from a literate class, he appears to have been a little defensive about his error. The presumably literate officers in command of the French and British armies that plundered the Chinese emperor's summer palace on 6 October 1860 do not appear to have been remorseful about their destruction of the 168,000 volumes in the palace library, particularly as Lord Elgin, the son of the famous despoiler of the Parthenon, resolutely returned on the 18th of the same month to finish off the job.

Nevertheless the illiterate do appear to have a particular loathing for the library, possibly because they know that they are excluded from its power. While other objects are looted, these useless and highly inflammable items are wilfully destroyed. Men of violence dislike books and bookishness, and on the whole books and bookishness return the compliment:

> Almighty Author and Lover of peace, scatter the nations that delight in war, which is, above all plagues, injurious to books. For wars being without the control of reason make a wild assault on everything they come across, and lacking the check of reason they push on without discretion or distinction to destroy the vessels of reason.[13]

The amiable, slightly pedestrian and decidedly peaceable Anglo-Norman Richard de Bury (1287-1345) wrote several chapters of his *Philobiblon* as though books themselves were speaking. This passionate bibliophile very possibly exaggerated in his deification of the written word, but all of us who detest war can join the books in their prayer as it appears in the English translation above.

Polastron, who has studied the matter in depth, feels that monotheist religions are particularly prone to book-burning. The evidence that this is so in the moments of military victory appears to be slim, as this can be considered a constant. These religions were however affected by a cycle of expansion and destruction for reasons of religious orthodoxy and purification, although Islam was the least affected, at least before the Enlightenment. A particularly distressing but instructive incident occurred in 1233 when orthodox Jews in Monpellier petitioned the Inquisitor for books by Maimonides to be burnt, and the zealous cleric decided to burn all Jewish books including the Talmud (of the three religions, Judaism is the one that invests most significance in the sacred nature of the written word; it is also worth noting that the works of Maimonides are now considered ultra-orthodox). For me the most terrible event described in Polastron's book does not involve a large number of books:

---

13. Richard de Bury, *Philobiblon* (Oxford: Basil Blackwell, 1960), p. 71. This bilingual text also contains the original Latin.

St. Cyril of Alexandria, who controlled a mob of Christian bigots, was allegedly responsible for having had Hypatia stoned to death with roof tiles. She was then cut into pieces which were then thrown on a fire along with all her books. Even if he was not personally responsible for her death, Saint Cyril, who also undertook to destroy the writings of the apostate Emperor Julian (apparently of literary worth), had organised a squad of five hundred bravoes who terrorised non-Christians in public spaces such as theatres and tribunals. These *parabalani* were the principal perpetrators of her murder. Hypatia, a philosopher and mathematician, was the daughter of Theon, the last of the philosophers of the Alexandrine Museum, and her death, which was in clear breach of Christ's injunctions and all the more scandalous because of the apparent innocence of the victim, demonstrates how bibliophobia can be a crowd-puller.

The wily Almanzor or al-Mansūr ("the victorious") came from humble origins, and literacy provided his initial career as a professional letter writer. His instinct for all aspects of politics from seduction or, at the very least, ingratiation of the caliph's favourite wife to the affairs of state and the art of war provided him with all the reins of power, although the young and ineffectual caliph Hishām II came to the throne in 976 AD and retained the title. This Machiavellian prince *avant la lettre* was profligate and not free from public criticism in the early part of his career. His infallible political instinct convinced him to do something he is unlikely to have approved of in principle: to burn the Caliph's library to please religious fanatics and the crowd. This unholy alliance of the powerful and the people has often destroyed accumulated knowledge throughout history, even though most literary works are overly deferential to the powerful (and also hostile to the "crowd", reflecting the innate conservatism of much of the intellectual class).

Almanzor would become the subject of a play that took his name; written by Heinrich Heine in 1821, it produced the famously prophetic line, "Where they burn books, they will in the end burn human beings too" – prophetic for the scale on which this observation of the past would come true in the future, and prophetic because Heine's own works were amongst those burned by the thousand in Berlin's Opernplatz in 1933.

China appears to lead the way in large-scale centrally organised destruction not only of its books but also its culture as a whole – a kind of auto-da-fé of the social mind. The most famous cases of this collective self-harming were the product of two extreme megalomaniacs intent upon massive programmes of modernisation, rationalisation and centralisation: Li Si in 213 BC and Chairman Mao Tse-Tung in 1966. Li Si was the Emperor Quin Shi Huang's demonic chancellor, and was more extreme than Almanzor. He ordered the systematic destruction of all historical records and philosophical works, including the works of Confucius himself, and had 460 Confucian scholars buried alive after they had protested. He felt that the learning of the past subverted the rule of ministers in the present. Mao's Cultural Revolution may not have produced as many deaths as the famines caused by Stalin's forced collectivization or the insane Great Leap Forward which Mao himself had organised in the 1950s, but its nightmarish creation of a society of humiliators and humiliated amounted to institutionalised hysteria. It was said that only five plays were considered suitable to be staged in Chinese theatres, and they were all written by Madame Mao. That might of course be Western propaganda or an "urban myth", but the story does seem quite typical of the frighteningly irrational and destructive forces at work, albeit in their most absurdist mode. Although both these regimes, which could be defined as dictatorships of the present, were to be short-lived, they changed China irreversibly and permanently destroyed cultural realities.

The hatred of books is both rational (ideas are dangerous) and irrational (books are mysterious and chaotic). The powerful have a rational dislike of books, which is mitigated by a rational awareness that some forms of learning are essential to the survival of a state. The "crowd" (a motley alliance of the orthodox, the fanatical and the illiterate) have an irrational dislike of books, which is associated with a whole series of prejudices against those "who got their learning from books". This prejudice is not without a tiny element of truth: writing, an extremely artificial act, does inevitably have a distorting effect, although nothing like as pronounced as that of film and television. The reason for this is, once again, that writing, although artificial, is closely associated to one of our most natural activities – speech.

After Gutenberg's invention of printing, it became difficult to understand why people had previously become so agitated about the written word; its real power was just about to be revealed. Previously, books were a restricted luxury item and very few people had the skill to decipher them, and so printing inevitably revolutionised the way we use and perceive them. In 1553, one hundred years after Gutenberg had completed the long process of inventing the printing press with moveable type, a man was burned at the stake with what was thought to be the last copy of his book strapped to his leg. One of the many distressing aspects of Michael Servetus's story is that he too probably thought that the book whose heresies burnt along with his own flesh would die with him, as the authorities of Calvin's Geneva fully intended. Servetus had consciously run a tremendous risk by publishing *Christianismi Restitutio* after twenty years living under a false name: there can be no doubt about the importance he attached to its survival.

He was reputed to have said, "Wretched am I who cannot end my life in this fire", as the slow-burning green wood tortured him with its flames. In the great slaughter-house called history, this image stands out like the one of a man dying on the cross. Like Christ, Servetus displayed all the behavioural patterns that are most likely to incense the scribes and pharisees of any religion: whether Catholic orthodoxy or reformed sects. He was a highly sensitive man whose ethical standards eschewed any personal ambition and who was profoundly concerned about the mistreatment of his Muslim and Jewish fellow-countrymen. What interests us here is that he also displayed the classic characteristics of the highly bookish intellectual who would become an increasingly significant figure as the flood of printed paper steadily and irreversibly changed Europe through centuries that followed. He was one of those exceptional individuals who would probably have achieved great learning even in earlier times: he knew Latin, Spanish, Catalan, French and probably some other vernaculars. He was an accomplished doctor and discovered the circulation of blood long before William Harvey published his findings in 1628 (this discovery was contained in his book and was burned with it, thus losing over seventy years for medical science). Most importantly for his religious studies, he was highly literate in Latin, Greek, Hebrew and Arabic, and was therefore capable of careful examination and collation of the scriptures of all three monotheist religions and of the translations of the Bible. Like many intellectuals, he believed very foolishly that most people, particularly fellow supporters of the reformed religion, were as interested as he was in rational argument and careful study. He thought that he could go around spouting off his idea of a more gentle religion free from the obvious absurdity of the trinity without unleashing the oppressive instincts of the magistratures of all the Protestant and Catholic states. There may have been a little vanity or even arrogance in Servetus's conviction that his superior intellect could convince others, but mostly there was a generosity of heart that made his end inevitable. Calvin and Luther were superb scholars too, but they were not natural scholars like Servetus; ambition drove them to scholarship so that they could use it for the attainment of power. Men and women who pursue learning as an end in itself are on their way to complete solitude, because on the whole, human beings are not designed for rational thought but for thought constricted by social context.[14]

The story of Servetus is particularly important in the history of publishing, because even in this extreme case in which all jurisdictions worked in unison, a startling thing occurred: three copies of this most reviled book survived and it would become clear (after some time, it has to be said) that printing had made the social mind almost indestructible. One surviving copy had belonged to Calvin himself, even though he had introduced a law imposing the death penalty for possession of the book. He clearly trusted himself with the toxic heresy, but could not choose the moment of his passing. Beyond the irony, what better demonstration could there be of the durability of the printed word. Writing had created a tangible but fragile part of the social mind; printing had removed that fragility.

---

14. Any attempt to break out of the solitude imposed by learning must be informed by the realisation that even in the most liberal state, there is always a cost – particularly in relation to politics, religion and ethics. In conformist eras such as the current one, the cost is bound to be higher, and this explains why modern journalism has become so toothless.

This was not the only innovation: the almost obsessive nature of the Calvin-Servetus rivalry must have been one of the first great literary feuds. Servetus's erudition took him effortlessly to the top and, in spite of being a very young man from a modest background, he was invited to Charles V's coronation as emperor in Bologna. Yet he was disgusted by the pomp and extravagance, and chose to turn his back on a promising career. Calvin, on the other hand, worked hard to make the right connections and initially appeared bent on a career within the Catholic Church in moderate reforming mode – an attempt to repeat Erasmus' dazzling publishing success. His first book – a further absurdity in this bizarre tale – was a plea for tolerance; paid for from his own limited funds, the book was an utter failure. However, copies of Servetus' first polemical tract jumped off the booksellers' shelves, even though the names of the author and printer could not be acknowledged because of the inflammatory nature of the content. In the new universe of the printed word, it was no longer just important what you wrote; it mattered when you got it published. The pace of debate had quickened. Calvin eventually had the courage to make the leap over to the reformed religion and achieved his publishing success with *Institutes of the Christian Religion*, but we are left with this nagging doubt: had the public reacted more favourably to Calvin's first work, would he have remained a Catholic?

And this was not the only literary spat: at the other end of the literary scale and at about the time Calvin had Servetus burnt to death, two ex-Augustinian monks turned inveterate hacks were demonstrating how vicious rivalries could be in the first Grub Street. Ludovico Domenichi was a rather pedestrian writer of anti-classical texts and his friend Anton Francesco Doni a spirited, eclectic and actually very talented writer, if we take into account the straitened circumstances in which such men had to work. Doni explained that he worked in the printer's workshop on four books at a time. When he had finished a page of one book he would hand it to the printers, and move on to the next book. Unsurprisingly his books did not stand out for the coherence of their structures. These were people who were barely making a living, not because their books weren't selling in large numbers but rather because they were working at the bottom end of the market where the margins were small. Doni's partnership with the printer Marcolini was particularly fruitful and his works were translated from Italian into other European vernaculars. Then Domenichi did the unforgivable: he plagiarised one of Doni's short stories. It was not a great work of literature, but these were men who had to produce text every day and occasionally they just had to cheat. Copyright law did not exist, and in any case, that would not have been Doni s style. He sent word to Piacenza, which Domenichi was about to visit, saying that a vicious heretic would soon arrive in the town. Domenichi was arrested and tortured, although fortunately he was released when the Inquisition eventually came to the conclusion that in this case their source had not been entirely reliable. The printing press turned up the volume, raised the stakes and, at the very least, changed the style of litigiousness.

Printing created the "intellectual" in the more general sense, rather than the intellectual member of a court or religious or administrative hierarchy. This new figure was a person of any class who used the greater access to the social mind to expand the individual mind in a manner that was not previously possible. "Intellectual" is, of course, an elusive concept like so many others, but I take it to mean the holder of a bookish knowledge affected by a certain detachment from reality or even impracticality, arising from an emphasis on reason in a society in which reason is not the dominant force. Pure intellectuals rarely make good politicians, although there are some notable exceptions. Although seekers of "reason", intellectuals are often extremely unreasonable in their professional and personal lives, as we have seen with Calvin and Servetus. Other famous spats included those between Hume and Rousseau, and between Hegel and Schopenhauer. Clearly intellectual pursuits were always attractive to human beings, but printing made this a real possibility not solely for an elite, but for great numbers of people from very different social backgrounds.

During the first half-century after Gutenberg, this widening of the subject matter suitable for books was not dramatic, because printers were satisfying the centuries-old demand for bibles and classical works by a small group of exalted writers, particularly Cicero and Virgil. Before printing, books were in danger not only from invading armies and the flaming torches of the intolerant mob, but also from the natural deterioration of the various substances on which text was written, all of which were made of organic matter (with the exception of clay bisques for cuneiform script). The business of copying by hand was so laborious that society was put under a considerable strain just maintaining the core religious, legal and medical texts. Initially publishers had plenty of work just satisfying this ancient demand, but around 1500, it became clear that their unimaginable success had saturated the market. Over the next sixty years, all the genres we would now recognise were developed by resourceful printer-publishers (the distinction between these two categories had not yet occurred). Of course, they drew on medieval literature with variations of the chivalric romance, and on classical literature, with a plethora of Platonic dialogues. All the time there was a shift from Latin to the vernacular, and the new genres started in the vernacular. In the early sixteenth century, only very self-confident languages, such as Italian (more correctly called the *Lingua Toscana*), leapt into such established genres as history. In the 1520s, they started to publish collections of letters, which obviously used all manner of speech because they were not written for publication (Machiavelli, for instance, wrote to an aristocratic friend and mentioned for no particular reason that "I was sitting on the bog [*cesso*] when they brought me your letter", which also says something about the familiar relationship between servants and masters at the time (it is unlikely today that an employee would hand his employer his mail while the latter was defecating, in spite of the enormous premium we put on an efficient use of time). Anti-classical satires enjoyed mimicking and ridiculing the great names of classical literature. The demotic was gradually making its way into literature. On a more practical level, publishers produced travel guides to help tourists and pilgrims, and collections of aphorisms on politics or literature taken from a wide range of writers so that the upwardly mobile could show off erudition they didn't really have.

Of course, contemporaries were well aware of the revolutionary nature of printing in the sixteenth century, and as with modern technology, feelings were mixed even amongst those who were most fascinated by this new reality. In the preface to his first book, the moderate Catholic reformist commentary on Seneca's books on clemency, Calvin wrote, "Whoever in this day has been born with more than average ability ... generally rushes out with it into the world, fired by the ambition of getting fame, so that posterity may venerate his memory with monuments to his genius ... Hence the insane passion to write something."[15] Aristocrats naturally disliked their territory being invaded, and Calmeta, one of

---

15. Quoted in Lawrence and Nancy Goldstone, *Out of the Flames* (New York: Broadway Books, 2002), p. 85.

the more vocal detractors, regretted the inflationary effect that devalued the currency of literature – he was probably thinking of such plebeians as Doni, but possibly also minor and impoverished nobles such as Calvin:

> But in this present age, presumptuous ambition reigns supreme because of the great availability of printers, so that, ignoring Horace's admonishment that says *et nonum prematur in annum*,[16] people get their works published as soon as they have finished them in order to claim a certain fame.[17]

Doni himself had a better measure of what was happening, but then he was amongst those writers whose ambition was simply to make a meagre living:

> And [...] this is a treadmill we are all happy to turn. Yet we paper-shitters [*schacazza-carte*] (who are obliged to do this) are driven by our madness to throw out something for the plebs to chew on every day. The truth is that there are those who prepare a better table, that is to say they provide a more tasty and nutritious food, and possibly more sticky and starchy too. But then this dining-table needs all qualities of meat in order to feed lords, gentlemen,

---

16. Calmeta slightly misquotes Horace's advice not to publish until the ninth year. The advice in full was: "But you will say nothing and do nothing against Minerva's will; such is your judgement, such your good sense. Yet if you ever do write something, let it enter the ears of some critical Maecius, and your father's, and my own; then put your parchment in the closet and keep it back till the ninth year. What you have not published you can destroy; the word once sent forth can never come back," Horace, *Ars Poetica*, lines 385-90, trans. by H. Rushton Farclough (London: Leob Classical Library, 1955). It is interesting to note the primacy of the spoken language at the time: the advice is not to let some expert critic read it, but to let him hear it.
17. *Prose e poesie edite e inedite*, ed. C. Grayson (Bologna: 1959), pp. 3-4.

women, workers, peasants and porters, because we are indebted to those who are knowledgeable and those who aren't.[18]

The greater availability of classical texts was to lead to their demise and a greater reliance on the observation of reality and the careful recording of its phenomena. If we take medical research as our example, we find that there was an increasing impatience with the works of Galen, previously considered the fountain of all reliable knowledge. Andreas Vesalus, the great Flemish anatomist who for a period taught at Padua University, would shout "leave your books!" (*via dai libri*) at his students. The more erratic and less successful German scholar Paracelsus would ritually burn copies of Galen and Avicenna. Printing was encouraging people to distrust established ideas and to observe from experience, often of course with the intention of writing down their own results. Indeed Vesalius was a prolific writer as well as an untiring researcher into the mechanics of the human body.

Doni, forever playing around and recording the chatter of his times for us, took up Vesalius' argument and, as ever, turned it into the absurd, "I have read that fire burns, but unless I touch it I will never know what fire is."[19] Indeed a jobbing literary buffoon like Doni left us with a great deal of technical information from the time. He wrote a popular handbook on music, which accounts for much of our knowledge of sixteenth-century music, and another one on painting and sculpture, about which he joked, "by my faith, I wouldn't know how to make a drinking-trough for chicks with a chisel, nor could I draw the head of a cricket, and yet, thanks be to God, I jabbered on for I don't know how many

---

18. Anton Francesco Doni, *La seconda libraria* (Venice: Marcolini, 1551), p. 6.
19. Doni, *I marmi* (Venice: Marcolini, 1553), II, p. 67.

pages."[20] With Doni you also get the weariness of the professional writer: "I haven't chewed on a piece of bread that wasn't sweated out of my brain." He loved to repeat that the fumes of the print-shop drove people mad with ambition. The first "mass medium" had arrived.

The written word may have been devalued by printing, but it was more powerful, because it was everywhere. As power depends on linguistic relationships (as argued in Chapter One), a sudden change in how language was used was bound to affect the stability of power. That printing was going to change politics and social organisation forever had been made clear by the success of the Reformation, whose ideas were fairly timid and even slightly reactionary, unlike many of the short-lived attempts at religious revival in the Middle Ages or indeed the contemporary social unrest in Germany. In German-speaking areas, the "broadsheet" was a large single-sheet, polemical and mass-circulation propaganda tool, and its effect was devastating. From now on there would be greater popular involvement in political conflict, and it seems reasonable to argue that printing contributed to the rise of nationalism because it both simplified the communication of ideas between different regions and coalesced peoples around a cultural standard (although this second factor remained fairly limited in its scope for three centuries). Because printing caused such a chaos of ideas, it was important for the authorities to control publishing, as we have seen in the case of Servetus. Of course, they were in part successful, although they often had to resort to draconian measures. As the printed word chipped away at the power structures and very slowly pushed the continent towards democracy, power discovered increasingly sophisticated methods for

20. Doni, *La seconda libraria*, ... p. 151. *Grillo*, the Italian word for "cricket", is also the word for "whim" or "fantastic notions".

counteracting the seditious nature of the printed word that did not involve outright repression. Power had to fight fire with fire, and so it used its greater resources to dominate the printed word.

As printing was a European invention and therefore at the heart of Christendom, the Bible played a significant role in the formation and survival of languages. Its translation was of course associated with Protestantism, although it was also translated in some Catholic countries, often by a protestant minority. Luther's translation was the most significant, while the English Bible had less influence on the language than might have been expected. The sixteenth-century translations of Slovenian and Welsh Bibles at least partly explain their better performance compared with other languages and "dialects" in their regions. Many mistakenly believe that the demise of Scots was principally due to the Union of the Crowns and the Union of Parliaments. Although those events and others certainly made their contribution, it was John Knox's decision to adopt the existing English translation rather than commission a Scots one that dealt the heaviest blow to the language that, with the steady contraction of Gaelic, was by then the most widely spoken in Scotland. Two centuries later, an English army officer visiting Edinburgh at the height of the Scottish Enlightenment noted that Hume, Smith and their set spoke and argued in Scots, and could communicate only in rather stilted English, the language of culture in which they expressed themselves on paper with some difficulty.[21] Had there been an authoritative Bible in Scots, they would very probably have been writing in Scots.

---

21. "Later in the 18th century the *literati* of the Scottish Enlightenment still spoke Scots but for writing they had developed an effective, but Latinate and sometimes ponderous, English prose." For this and the interesting quote from the English officer, see Paul Henderson Scott, *Andrew Fletcher and the Treaty of Union* (Edinburgh: Saltire Society, 1992) p. 69.

The standardising influence of the printed word also made its presence felt in early sixteenth-century secular literature. Italy was the country in which secular publishing was most developed, and within that world, Venice was the centre of this new industry. They had a problem, however. They needed a standard that would be acceptable to all literate Italians. Because of the widely acknowledged pre-eminence of Tuscan or, perhaps more specifically, Florentine literature, it was accepted the solution had to lie in that direction, but as language changes over time as well as geographically, this did not solve the problem. The Venetian cardinal, Pietro Bembo, who produced the industry standard, had to choose from three contenders: sixteenth-century Florentine (the language used by Machiavelli and Guicciardini), courtly Tuscan (the language used in the various courts of Italy, largely based on Tuscan/Florentine) or fourteenth-century, "classical" Florentine (the language of Boccaccio in prose and Petrarch in poetry). He chose this last "classical" version, probably because it had greater authority, and it was indeed remarkably successful in establishing itself in a short time as literary Italian and much later as the national language of Italy. Paradoxically, Florentine writers were the most dissenting group and continued to write in their own modern version, while writers outside Tuscany wrote in a Florentine that was no longer spoken. Ludovico Ariosto had already published two versions of his famous poem, *Orlando furioso*, when his third and final version came out in 1532, and this one fully conformed to Bembo's dictates. The relationship he had with this new language must have been very similar to that of David Hume with standard English, but he lived in a more complex linguistic world. He was trilingual at the very least: he would have spoken an upper-class version of *emiliano*, Latin and a variant of Tuscan that acted as a lingua franca. He would also have had more than a nodding acquaintance with Venetian and some other European languages required for his diplomatic activities. The idea of the clearly defined national language was still far off, but printing had started pushing European societies in that direction.

Printing was ultimately the cause of the increasing intolerance of the Modern Era. Historians currently perceive medieval men and women as fundamentally different from ourselves. Of course, they were different and also very different amongst themselves. However, it is wrong, I think, to consider them to be universally orthodox in their religious and philosophical views. In many ways, the Middle Ages were quite liberal: Augustinian and Thomist views, which would be claimed by Protestants and Catholics respectively, co-existed in the medieval Church after Aquinas. More importantly, there is evidence of widespread heretical views and atheism, which were occasionally repressed with great ferocity, although there was usually another good political reason for doing so. Dante put a cardinal in hell for famously believing in the mortality of the soul: this does not appear to have interfered with the cleric's career in the Church. Popular writers of the first half of the sixteenth century spoke of people who "did not believe in anything above the rooftops". The expression was recorded by printing, but there is no reason to believe that such expressions did not predate Gutenberg. Printing now covered a much wider range of language than before, but the spoken language was still immeasurably richer in dialects, registers and surely matters suitable for discussion.

Thus printing introduced us to a new world that was decidedly more dogmatic (previously people had been willing to murder each other on a grand scale out of loyalties to a network ultimately based on the family unit and vassalage, now they were also willing to do this out of loyalties to rigid and abstract ideas), less reverential (the written word lost its mystery and so did the power of the literate), more knowledgeable (the social mind continued to expand exponentially and no one could hold it back through acts of destruction), more conflictual (social movements could spread their ideas more easily), and above all more wordy. A historical trend had been reversed: not for a long time had the word enjoyed such power and imparted such pleasure, albeit in a new and somewhat artificial form. Humanity had rediscovered its innate garrulousness and the fumes of the printer's workshop were indeed driving it mad.

Of course, technological development did not end there. The development of film and more especially television in the twentieth century has undermined the importance of the written word. Many people are now more accustomed to having stories told to them in images. This creates two fundamental problems I have already mentioned. Firstly, we have not been designed by nature to assimilate our stories through images and there may therefore be some kind of psychological deficit. In other words, the written or printed word may be artificial but it relates to an instinctive activity, but the moving picture's artificiality is wholly alien to our way of thinking, although those who have lived with it all their lives undoubtedly develop a sophisticated understanding of the moving image. Secondly, film and television are capable of great art, but cannot produce the ethical, psychological and philosophical nuances that can be produced by the written word. The result is that a story can rest entirely on its visual impact and lose all its explanatory purpose. This produces powerful results in terms of the generational transference of moral concepts and ways of understanding. Some of these consequences have been positive and other negative, but the more general result may be a more superficial and fragmented society.

In spite of all the hype, computers have probably had less effect than television. Essentially computers have taken the development of the social mind and the atrophy of the individual mind one stage further. Doctor Johnson wrote that there are two kinds of knowledge: what we know and what we know how to find out. The computer and the internet have considerably increased our access to information (perhaps not always very reliable information). The computer has increased the tangibility of the social mind, and some might think that immediate access to information through human memory almost redundant. But it is precisely the oceanic vastness of the Internet that lessens its potency. The blogosphere records society's chatter on an unprecedented scale, but its superabundance and amorphousness are both exhilarating and self-defeating. Blogs and e-mail may well be finishing off the process whereby the written word increasingly resembles the spoken word, but what is understandably inarticulate in the spoken language becomes unnecessarily indolent in the written one. Of one thing we can be sure, recent technological developments have shattered the supremacy of the word, which reached its zenith in the first four centuries of printing. Inasmuch as the word remains powerful, it is because it is so intimately connected to the essence of what it is to be human.

Chapter Five

Big is not beautiful, but merely more profitable

The PhD student in agricultural management set out early in the morning to discover the wild and alien nature of the land in which he found himself. He was glad to be alone. The students' hostel was a dull place and the other students stiff and unapproachable. He missed his own climate, but he had to admit the bracing air was strange, exhilarating and not unpleasant. He skirted the lake and began to climb the foothills, taking whichever path attracted him most. The day wore on, and pleasure turned to tiredness. The way back did not seem entirely clear. Like most inhabitants of sub-Saharan Africa, he knew three "native" languages. They were called native by the Europeans to imply simplicity, paucity and ease-of-learning. In reality they were not closely related and were dense with different interpretations. He also spoke perfect French, passable English and poor Russian, which only confirmed the prejudices of those of his fellow students who were Russians. Just before tiredness turned to exhaustion and uncertainty over his bearings turned to panic, he noticed the bar just outside the village that led back to the college. It was a grey box of a building with a flat roof and jutting shelter, the only non-utilitarian element presumably added as a feeble gesture of homage to modernism and the defiance of reinforced concrete. The only colour on its side was a chipped enamel advert for a certain cigarette, on which a young woman smiled from another age with other tastes in fashion. Her busty form and blond hair spoke of an aesthetics of female beauty that had been replaced several times by other modish international standards, none of which ever consulted the people of this area or any other. He knew of the bar. The students avoided it, because it was preferred by the indigenous Votyak-speakers. Driven by his desire for rest, he entered. By the time his eyes had adjusted to the poor lighting, a group of well-built regulars were marching towards him. He froze, unsure of their intentions. Their hands grabbed his arms and lifted him physically. And then came a rush of incomprehensible words. The universal language of laughter surrounded him as they pressed him to the bar and poured him an absurd quantity of vodka. They pointed upwards to intimate his jaunt in the hills, and he realised that in such a small place nothing went unnoticed by these people who were sealed into the privacy of their own language. He nodded, grinned and started to speak in his own Ekoi. It was the first time in many months that he had heard words in his own tongue spoken aloud, and they expressed an isolation that the others would surely comprehend. What did it matter that one person did not understand the other? Their words were only colour and sound, and he knew them to be friendly.

Perhaps one of the most amusing accounts of how the new story-telling in pictures coupled with universal education was always going to challenge our linguistic diversity is a passage from Doctor Donald Macdonald's *Tales and Traditions of the Lews*. George Mikes said that the English do not have a soul, they have understatement, but clearly he had never met the Gaels who build their subtle humour precisely on their use of extreme understatement. MacDonald, who died in 1961, did not live long enough to see the advent of television on his native Lewis, and perhaps it was a good thing that he too was not obliged to witness how his prescient fears would turn into depressing realities:

We have now further education for the adult; men

do not work so long, and so have more free time at their disposal, and the modern inventions, the radio and the movie van, are reaching out to every village in Lewis. Most of our natives are suspicious of what these two may bring. Will they upset their ways, and interfere with their religious beliefs, which many believe are the only real and true beliefs? I fear them more in case they are hastening the departure of our dear Gaelic language, for the searchings and probings into the wonders of the Creator will refuse to be stilled or thwarted; and I fear that in the future this go-getting Anglo-Saxon language will be the one in which these mysteries will be unfolded to the bodachs [old men] of Bragar, Brue and Brenish.[1]

MacDonald was right. Language is not only the most important part of human culture; it is also the most unstable and fragile. The question is: what is also lost when a community loses its language?

When printing was invented, there was either an infinity of languages or merely a handful according to your definition of a language. Latin was a language in the more restricted sense of the term, because, although people disagreed over what correct Latin was, they accepted that there was such a thing as correct Latin – a norm from which no one was supposed to deviate. English on the other hand was not a language in this sense, but a myriad of related vernaculars or "parlances" (to avoid that misleading word "dialects"). There was not complete equality between these vernaculars, as those spoken by the most powerful families or in the most powerful cities would be more prestigious, but over the centuries the fortunes of these vernaculars would

---

1. Donald MacDonald, *Tales and Traditions of the Lews* (Edinburgh: Birlinn, n.d.), p. 221.

change with the changing fortunes of the families or cities that spoke them. Thus in one century, the most prestigious vernacular was the Northumbrian one and in another century it was the Wessex one, always remembering that these "dialects" would themselves be fragmented into many often quite distinct vernaculars.

Before printing and for some time afterwards, it did not matter greatly what language was spoken by the peasantry. Indeed, under feudalism the aristocracy preferred to speak a different language to that of the peasantry. Thus the Norman aristocracy in England spoke Norman-French to distinguish itself from the people who herded the cattle and sheep but rarely ate *boeuf* and *mouton*, while the Anglo-Norman aristocracy in Scotland spoke English to distinguish themselves from the Gaelic peasantry. But as ideas began to circulate, everybody's language became a matter of concern to central government. After many long centuries first of Norman and then of English dominance, the Welsh language suddenly became a political issue in the late nineteenth century and the reasons were pretty clear. Welsh, like English, now had a standard used in the written language, although most Welsh people, like most English people, continued to speak in their own way. The continued vitality of the Welsh language threatened the security of the principality and the ability to integrate the region into the dominant culture. A parliamentary commission did not attempt to hide its hostility and suggested that the Welsh language had to be completely obliterated in the interests of political stability. The modern world does not like diversity, although the trend towards homogenisation around a select group of languages goes back a long way.

One family of languages has been successful beyond measure. It originated somewhere in Central Asia and expanded southwards into northern India and Persia, and westwards into Europe. There it wiped out all indigenous languages with the exception of Basque. This does not mean that we all descend from the Indo-Europeans, but it does mean that we carry their linguistic DNA. Nor does it mean that Indo-European languages were superior to others; it merely means that the military prowess and perhaps the cruelty of the invaders who spoke these languages were greater than those of the other peoples. From Europe, it expanded even further on the back of European colonialism. Of the imperial languages, French, Spanish, Portuguese, English and Russian, the first three are neo-Latin, and the fourth is a Germanic and neo-Latin mix. In this sense, European empire can be seen as an extension of the Roman one. Hindi, another Indo-European language, and three large non-Indo-European languages, Arabic, Mandarin Chinese and Malaysian/Indonesian are putting up some resistance to European domination, but they too are slayers of the languages beneath them in the political hierarchy they command.

This steady expansion over the last four or five millennia has been a disaster for the world's linguistic variety. But up until recently there was at least the possibility of generating new languages. All these great imperial languages are recent inventions of the millennium that has just ended. Russian is a very recent creation, and the others mostly an invention of the printing press and dynastic happenstance. The decline of the world's remaining 6,000 languages is now dramatic. Currently, English is rising up like a terrifying behemoth that devours other languages by sucking them dry and tanning their skins so that they can be sold to the tourists. English is the quintessential bourgeois language: the language of trade, in an age when trade has become absolute power. It is linear and shallow. It is brittle and often smug. It is practical and often sensible. It is difficult to write in, because it is too easy to write in, while not lending itself to saying difficult things. It presents the writer with the challenge of its limitations, and limits the reader by its economic power and ubiquity.

The simplicity of English grammar and the rigidity of its syntax are useful to its role as a lingua franca, but at the same time increase its danger: English turns everything it touches to stone. Once English had a certain vibrancy, and the English themselves attempted to learn other languages. Now English forces itself on the world and the Anglophone has no interest of expressing himself outside his own vast linguistic domain. It is the new Latin, but lacks Latin's subtlety or rather it has a different kind of subtlety. It lacks ornate, circuitous and taxing thought processes, but because of its vastness it has created an enormous body of cross-references, dead metaphors and widely known quotations. Its vocabulary is rigid but also subtle and precise. These strengths and weaknesses, or more specifically these limitations and more refined tools provide an endless source for writers, but also suggest that the language is prematurely ageing. Normally a language when it reaches this stage suddenly enters a period of rapid metamorphosis, and like the Phoenix, rises anew out of its ashes, as the neo-Latin languages rose out of Latin. But the modern media do not allow for change. The British and American empires have not created new languages based on English (except in Papua New Guinea); the language remains remarkably homogeneous throughout its global domain, and that process of homogenisation continues apace. Nevertheless, it is still a pleasure to write in this language, and as is so often the case with creative activities, the limitations provide the challenge and therefore the gratification.

The problem of English is not unique, but only a more extreme example of the steady and quickening eclipse of smaller languages by larger ones. The destruction of Tibetan by Chinese and of Quechua by Spanish is the same tragedy as the destruction of Celtic, Native American and Aboriginal languages by English.

An Anglophone intellectual has said that a small minority language is only a code, which is like saying a small bird is a fish or a small tree is an insect. A language is a language and cannot be invented, and a code is a code and has to be invented. More than anything a language resembles a living being like an animal or a plant. It can be subject to intervention by man. Small committees and bureaucrats can alter a language, restrain it and push it in certain directions, just as animals can be bred and plants nurtured, grafted and trained, but languages cannot be invented out of nothing, in spite of the undoubtedly heroic efforts of Zamenhof and his elegant Esperanto. Ultimately a language takes its sustenance from its speakers, its history, its societies and its cultures. A language that has only two speakers left is going to die, but it still contains a vast range that goes far beyond those two people and their experience. On the other hand, a code could be invented by the cleverest of men and perfected by someone else, and it would still be nothing in comparison to the wealth of the dying language. Of course, a language will rapidly lose breadth as it falls below a few hundred speakers, particularly if they are geographically scattered, but even in the 20,000 odd words left in the dying brain cells of the very last speaker, there will be a mass of sayings, semantic distinctions, confusions, comedic methods and phonological prejudices that, even half remembered, will be a much greater edifice than anything that can be invented through the most complex code in the world.

It has been estimated that only 10% of the world's languages are likely to survive this century.[2] Of course these figures are only approximate, but given the enormity of

2. Michael Kraus's figure is quoted in David Crystal, *Language Death* (Cambridge: C.U.P., 2000), p. 18. On pages 4-18, Crystal discusses the various estimates for the number of languages in the world before coming up with his "off-the-cuff" figure of 6,000. The two figures imply that only 600 languages will survive.

the catastrophe they predict, even if it were a gross over-estimation, there would still be a terrible and irreversible impoverishment of our cultural resources. The rationalist mind often abhors the unknowable, and the sheer magnitude of human linguistic expression terrifies. Rationalism is commendable, and I wish we were better at it, but its arrogance (particularly when associated with power) has been satirised in many dystopian novels. It often demands that everything runs in accordance with its own economies. Thus language diversity in the modern age has been considered an unnecessary financial and intellectual cost and an obstacle to the smooth running of society. Rationalism abhors pointless effort, because of its love of efficiency. Nothing could be more philistine, although nothing could be more justifiable when resources are dangerously low. What monoglot intellectuals don't understand is that multilingualism does not actually require much effort. Much is made of the small army of translators and interpreters needed to keep the E.U. bureaucracy going, when in reality it is fairly streamlined and its costs infinitesimal compared with the potential financial *and cultural* costs of transforming Europe into a monoglot or at least less polyglot state. Much is made of the cost of Gaelic television, but its costs are tiny in a sector known for its high spending. Moreover, the process of multilingualism produces cultural benefits, as I have attempted to demonstrate.

The first thing we have to do, therefore, is to establish exactly what we would be losing, if we were to allow our language diversity to disappear. The immediate answer, of course, is that no one really knows because even the most accomplished linguist can only scratch the surface of this wonderful, chaotic multitude of complexities. We can, however, turn the argument around and state that no language can do everything. Ezra Pound wrote, "The sum of human wisdom is not contained in any one language, and no single language is capable of expressing all forms and degrees of human comprehension."[3] This is not simply because no language has yet reached perfection; it is inherent in the nature of language. Languages have character, and character always means denial of other traits. It is not primarily a question of vocabulary, because vocabulary is the most adaptable part of language, and words can be constantly borrowed (but you need the wealth of other languages from which to borrow, and a reasonable degree of awareness of other languages in a particular language community in order to provide a channel for inter-cultural exchange). The essential point is that languages are structurally different, and their different mechanisms affect the way speakers interpret the world. Of course, languages are all vast and sensitive creatures, so they can express an enormous range of concepts, ideas and emotions in various styles and registers, but the subtleties are never quite the same.

Every language is associated with a social mind, and thus if you destroy a language you destroy a social mind. If we take as our example Tasmania, whose language (or set of related languages) the British destroyed along with its entire population in a very short period, we can be sure that this one depressingly typical event also destroyed an intimate understanding of the Tasmanian environment, unique religious beliefs, oral literature and some kind of philosophical system.[4] Even if everything had been recorded in English, it would no longer be what it was. We have no means of assessing what we have lost, but we can be sure of its enormous value, because no human society has ever failed to produce

---

3. Ezra Pound, *ABC of Reading* (London: Faber and Faber, 1961), p. 34.
4. It took the British from 1803 to 1835 to destroy almost all the Tasmanian population, and the last Tasmanian died in 1876. Matthew Kneale's *English Passengers* provides an excellent satire of the administrative, religious and racial prejudices that contributed to this tragic destruction.

a wealth of ideas, which have parallels with those of other societies but also certain unique features.

In many cases, destruction was not so sudden, but rather a slow strangulation. Gaelic has been losing ground for almost a millennium. In the late sixteenth century, there was a dramatic change for the worse. James V was the last Scottish monarch to speak the language, and his grandson James VI started the political campaign to extirpate the language now called Erse and considered something foreign (Irish and therefore also Catholic). Gaelic was a literate language that also had strong oral traditions, but printing in the language arrived relatively late in the mid-eighteenth century. The political upheavals of that century destroyed the ancient linguistic social traditions and sparked off a flowering of poetic works in a language closer to the spoken one. On the other hand the manuscript tradition suffered: I read that the historical records kept by generations of the MacMhuirich chroniclers were being used by a descendant turned cobbler to stuff the soles of the shoes he made. Of course, not everything can be recorded. The problem is not the attrition, but the lack of regeneration.

In peasant society, multilingualism and learning were a treasured resource, even though human life was held cheap. MacDougall of Kilmun, a member of the MacDonald garrison in Kintyre when it fell to the Campbells in 1647, is reputed to have saved himself from the ensuing massacre of all the other prisoners-of-war by shouting in five languages, "Is there anyone here at all who will save a good scholar?"[5] Perhaps the best literary representation of the clash between a modern centralised monoglot state and a multilingual pre-industrial society is Brian Friel's *Translations*, a play about a troop of British sappers working in Ireland and their impact

---

5. See David Stevenson, *Highland Warrior. Alasdair MacColla and the Civil Wars* (Edinburgh: Saltire Society, 1994), p. 237.

on a rural area. There is inevitably a lack of understanding on both sides, but the greatest inability to understand is on the part of the centralised state, because it does not have to understand; indeed it must evade understanding at all costs. An understanding of the society it wishes to homogenise would undermine its entire imperial project. On the other hand, the society that is impacted wants to learn, as it immediately understands that even its partial survival depends on it. Friel manages to represent all this on stage with wit and precision. It reminds me of a comment by the great Dreyfusard intellectual, Bernard Lazare, on how racism is always the same whilst its victims' reactions are always entirely different, "Out in society, in the street, at the theatre and in the restaurant, there is the fear of hearing the word that has become an insult, and feeling it thrown in one's face; the jolt when confronted with a mocking or venomous look, in which one can read the affront and fear its utterance. And day after day all this grazes the skin, wearing down Jewish nerves, tearing at their hearts if they are sensitive, increasing their disdain if they are intellectuals and increasing their desire for violence and vendetta if they are hot-tempered."[6] Friel's Irish peasants also react in a wide variety of ways to the inevitability of change: hostile pragmatism, hopefulness, disdain to counter disdain, adaptation, violence. The British soldier who identifies with the Irish becomes the inevitable victim and the cause of further suffering for the people; in this game the perpetrators have fewer choices. Classical and modern empires are not so much interested in destroying people as in destroying cultures, although they did and still do a fair bit of the former. Medieval and territorial empires of the Modern Era appear to have thrived on a maintenance of linguistic diversity, and

6. Bernard Lazare, *Il letame di Giobbe* (Milan: Medusa, 2004) p. 59 (Original title: *Le fumier de Job*, Paris: 1928).

I will attempt to look at this in greater detail in my chapter on lingua francas (Chapter Seven).

Those intellectuals who are typically *bien pensant* would never be so politically incorrect as to dismiss "peasant" languages as barbaric or crude – they prefer to think of them as provincial, restricted, uneconomic and incapable of adapting to the modern world. I will deal with these assertions individually further on, but for the moment I want to concentrate on the problems of cultural hegemony created by the dominant-minority relationship.

You would expect racists, nationalists, religious bigots (where there is a linguistic dimension to a religious divide) and right-wing thinkers in general to be intolerant of linguistic minorities; what is surprising is that a great number of left-wing intellectuals also despise minority cultures. Marx is perhaps as good an example as any. The founding father of "scientific socialism" wrote, "There is no country in Europe that does not possess, in some remote corner, at least one remnant people, left over from an earlier population, forced back and subjugated by the nation which later became the repository of historical development."[7] Marx goes on to list some examples of this "national refuse", condemned to a reactionary role in history: the Gaels of Scotland, the Bretons of France and the Basques of Spain (an interesting assertion now we know the Basques put up the strongest resistance to Franco and the Bretons distinguished themselves against Nazi occupation, while so much of France did not).[8] Minorities mess up the political map of

---

7. Karl Marx, *The Revolutions of 1848* (London: Penguin: 1973), p. 221.
8. Some Breton nationalists sided with the Nazis, and this betrayal by a minority of the minority was used against the language in the post-war period – to great effect. Breton still has many speakers, but its age demography is dramatic. The language is destined to die within decades unless very radical action is taken.

Europe, and intellectuals often consider these untidy realities irrational.

Now we have supposedly moved into a multi-cultural
era, this monolithic concept of the nation-state should be
a thing of the past. It would appear that the "man-in-the-
street" is ahead of writers, politicians and journalists on
this point, and has little trouble with a layered national
identity that allows for multiple allegiances with realities
inwith and outwith national boundaries. While non-Welsh-
speaking Welsh intellectuals will often complain that the
Welsh language challenges their sense of national identity,
there is little evidence that the majority of their compa-
triots are so uncharitable. At the time of the 1991 census,
18.7% of the Welsh population was Welsh-speaking, but a
survey in 1995 showed that 88% of the whole population
felt pride in Welsh and 83% thought public bodies should
be bilingual. Moreover, 68% of non-speakers agreed with
the aim of enabling "the language to become self-sustain-
ing and secure as a medium of communication in Wales".
In 1996 a nation-wide Scottish survey showed that 86%
supported the view that "the Gaelic language and way of
life should be maintained" (a remarkable 56% strongly
agreed and a further 30% slightly agreed, while only 5%
disagreed).[9] However, a 1998 survey carried out in the
Western Isles, Skye and Lochalsh "support[ed] the view
that there is a minority group (around 10% of the population) that are much less likely to see the Gaelic language,
art and culture as playing a key role in the areas of social
and economic development. These individuals appear to
be heavily represented in the upper reaches of the professional, business and public sector hierarchies, areas where
many decisions affecting the evolving role of the language

---

9. *Report on Attitudes to the Gaelic Culture* (Edinburgh: System Three Scotland,
13 March 1996). This report was prepared for Cànan Limited in Skye.

will be taken".[10] In other words, the powerful, who are predominantly monoglots, are hostile to bilingualism. It is difficult for them to admit that something they do not have is of any worth, such is the intoxicating hubris of power. But publicly their arguments are, of course, couched in the restrained and evasive language of compassionate pragmatism ("we fully understand your justified demands, but unfortunately due to a lack of resources …").

Recently, however, there was one notable exception: Tessa Jowell speaking to a group of highly respectable (perhaps too respectable) Gaelic-language professionals, blithely announced that Gaels could not expect much because, unlike the Welsh, they had failed to protest with sufficient vociferousness. The Welsh television channel, S4C, was, according to her, part of a settlement with the then Conservative government at the time of a "sharp and even violent increase" in Welsh nationalism, which has been lacking in Scotland. This was tantamount to inviting her listeners to prepare their Molotov cocktails or, at the very least, go on hunger strike. As an exponent of non-violent action, I know that power very rarely concedes anything on the basis of justified and rational argument, but for a minister of state to admit this to her public reveals her belief that political cynicism is now a universally shared credo. Although no one can deny the crassness and indeed incongruity of a government minister putting such an argument to an interest group, it is perhaps uncharitable to criticise her for candour so untypical of New Labour, and she did introduce this part of her speech by saying, "This'll irritate you, I suspect."[11] And her statement

---

10. Alan Sproull and Douglas Chalmers, *The Demand for Gaelic Artistic and Cultural Products and Services: Patterns and Impacts* (Glasgow: Caledonian University, March 1998).

11. Keynote Speech to the Celtic Media Festival held in Portree on Friday 30 March 2007. See the CMF website and webcast of speech at: http://strea ming portal.multistream.co.uk/celticmediafestival/pres14/wm_pres14.htm

is quite correct: the rights of minority languages have to be fought for, and even the smallest crumbs are only obtained after considerable personal sacrifices.

In the sixties, a Welsh sub-postmistress lost her license and livelihood for replacing the POST OFFICE sign above her shop with another saying SWYDDFA POST, and a fellow-countryman of hers had his furniture and moveables seized by bailiffs on several occasions because he refused to pay his rates until he received the bill in Welsh. It is better for these movements to arise from the courage and bloody-mindedness of the grass roots, but it should never spill over into intolerance of the majority: for as we have seen, the majority of the majority is often well-disposed towards the minority and, although obviously less passionate about the question, they too have a role to play in the defence of minority cultures. The torch should not be lit, but equally the minority should not feel that it cannot signal its existence to the majority. In 1996, there was a bizarre debate in the pages of Stornoway's local press over whether a new industrial estate should or should not have a Gaelic name. Some councillors felt that this could discourage inward investment. To be fair to the Labour administration in Scotland, this absurd timidity has now gone and the Gaelic Language Act (2005) has given Gaelic official status but, on the other hand, the financial resources that Gaelic taxpayers need and deserve have not been forthcoming. A linguistic minority that does not say or indeed shout, "I am here", is a linguistic minority that is fated to disappear.

One of the accusations against minority languages is that they are provincial and irretrievably cut off from the metropolitan centre, as though there was no communication between the two worlds. The sociolinguist Joshua Fishman has argued, "It is in the very nature of mainstream life to be unknowingly provincial and self-centred (while ascribing such traits only to others, who are outside the mainstream)."[12] Most speakers of minority languages are now also speakers of the dominant language. They therefore enjoy just as much access to the wider global community as the monoglot speakers of their dominant language, but they also have an added dimension. There is a confusion between the provincial and the periphery. In a sense everywhere is potentially part of the periphery – that is everywhere that remains true to its roots, everywhere that is not globalised. Periphery is distant from power, and again that distance cannot simply be measured in miles. But the periphery is not necessarily provincial; indeed provincialism is today as pronounced in the centre as it is the periphery, for provincialism is another concept that is not bound by physical distances. Provincialism, if it has any meaning at all, signifies an inability to look beyond one's own restricted cultural boundaries. It is the inability to conceive of other ways of doing things, and the ability to despise the products of those different perceptions and methods. Provincialism is the antithesis of art.

Because people confuse the periphery with provincialism, they fail to appreciate the artistic achievement of the periphery. Of the Italian writer Ignazio Silone who famously defined himself as "a Christian without a Church and a socialist without a party", Albert Camus wrote, "Look to Silone. He belongs utterly to his land, and yet is so completely European". The land that Silone belonged to was the desperately poor, malarial region around Matera in southern Italy where, like Scotland, land was owned by large estates. He was one of many European intellectuals in the interwar years who managed the difficult trick of being rooted in their ancestral past and adopting a sincerely internationalist outlook at the same time (something which is now much harder

---

12. Joshua Fishman, *Reversing Language Shift* (Clevedon: Multilingual Matters, 1991), p. 65.

to do). Sorley MacLean is another example: in *Hallaig* he imagines the bygone Gaelic community continuing to live in some parallel dimension of time, and yet his communism and internationalism also pervade his poetry. Silone, one of the founders of the Italian Communist Party, expresses the sense of his peasant roots in a dialogue between grandmother and grandson:

> "Poor child," says the grandmother; "how have you managed to survive such exertions with your delicate health?"
>
> "You see, grandmother," he replies, "I am one of those who has weak flesh and strong bones. A draught between two doors is enough to endanger my life, but a shipwreck has no effect on me at all."
>
> "And you know why?" she asks him. "During the worst adversities you had to endure, you never gave up because in the resistance that came from your bones you were joined by your ancestors – generations of diggers, vine-dressers, ploughmen and labourers, all hardened by bad weather and hard work."

The most common form of provincialism in these days of easy travel is not geographical provincialism but temporal provincialism: the inability to see beyond one's own time and its fashionable truths. For this reason, the periphery tends to be less provincial; it is more aware of itself as a historical entity, and that sense of continuity for which it has so long been berated becomes its strength, its ability not to be blown with every passing idea or vogue. New ideas are good, but only if they are tempered through comparison with ideas of the past and ideas of elsewhere. And not if they are held up as deified truths in a society that is terrified of dissent. The periphery with its linguistic and cultural particularities, however threatened, can judge innovation from a position where there still remains a modicum of *otium*, the untranslatable Latin word that denotes the inactivity necessary for collecting ideas and assessing one's reality (interestingly *negotium*, the Latin for "business" or "trade" and the root for our word "negotiate", comes from *nec otium*, "not *otium*", which suggests that the Romans saw this reflective activity as the primary activity and the opposite of making money, and making money is the only activity to which any value is attributed in the West today). The slower pace of the periphery and its greater garrulousness allows it to develop different ideas and different perspectives.

However, we should remember that this does not mean that the periphery is never provincial. When I mentioned the plight of Quechua speakers to an employee of a Gaelic organisation, I was horrified to hear him say that he was only concerned with Gaelic's survival, and the survival of other endangered languages was for him a matter of complete indifference. When I pointed out that it would be impossible to seek the support of non-Gaelic speakers if we lacked the same empathy we demand of others, the logic of this argument appeared entirely lost on him. Yet the Highlands and its cruel history have many stories that are relevant to the world today, in which clearances of culturally diverse groups continue relentlessly. The Quechuan Indians are being driven off their lands, as are the people of Chiapas and many other areas (I mention these examples because they so closely parallel the story of the Highlands, but of course even more tragic and very different events occur elsewhere – you only have to think of Darfur). Factors and policemen burn down miserable dwellings to make way for extensive agriculture and the displaced people drift, usually on foot, towards the burgeoning favelas and shanty towns outside some Third-World metropolis. To mourn the Highland Clearances is pointless self-indulgence if not accompanied by anger at these new clearances. Although I find the revisionist attempts to exonerate landlords like the Duke of Sutherland distasteful, I find equally distasteful the ritual bemoaning of our ancestors' fate while failing to understand the message of the story that should speak to us powerfully across two intervening centuries. I also hear people say the clearances have no relevance in the modern world, and perhaps their argument has some weight if we approach the question from a provincial viewpoint, but if we study the clearances in their wider context, then they have never been more relevant. Perhaps the saddest example of our failure to learn from the past came when our government encouraged Turkey to build a dam to flood the Kurdish-speaking area in its south-east. Undoubtedly clearance by water is even more effective than clearance by sheep.

Nor should we forget that some of the centre's advantages are perennial, because it offers dissenters the anonymity that permits original thought. The periphery may be happily distant from national government, but the local elite is always uncomfortably pervasive and often distinguished by extreme provincialism and indeed small-mindedness. In effect, the periphery is perhaps best seen as the nation's cultural seedbed: it generates the artists and intellectuals who then have to escape the conformism of the local power group, at least for a time. The point is perhaps best made, albeit unwittingly, by a Scottish intellectual who is known for his disapproval of assistance for Gaelic. Writing in *Scotland on Sunday* some years ago,[13] William McIlvanney refers to the

---

13. "Money alone can't pump life into a dying language", *Scotland on Sunday*, 17 September 2000, p. 19. McIlvanney, like many others, believes that there is a natural world for languages, and that "worthy intentions", "creative agendas", lobbies, committees and legislation do not save languages. But they do. Only military events have a more dramatic effect.

strengths of the English poetry produced by the Gaelic writer Ian Chrichton Smith, which in his opinion carries through something of the Gaelic flavour of Smith's background. This is supposed to show how English is a perfectly reasonable literary space for us all to participate in. Few would argue with his claim, but they might with his conclusion that everyone should simply move over to English. He appears to overlook the fact that, if Gaelic is allowed to die, it will no longer be possible for future Ian Chrichton Smiths to engage in such cross-fertilisation between languages, because Scotland will be an entirely monolingual society, at least as far as its "indigenous" languages are concerned. His argument is even stranger, because he is a highly accomplished author and inspired storyteller who writes much of his dialogue in Scots, about whose fate he is understandably concerned. Indeed he is a good example of what I am talking about. The mining community of Kilmarnock, into which McIlvanney was born in 1936, was at the time just as peripheral as the Gaelic-speaking communities to the north, because, as I have said, the periphery is a social distance not primarily a geographical one. He too brings to English his unique linguistic history.

This leads to another important point: where is Kilmarnock now, in this post-industrial age? Is the West becoming all centre and no periphery, such is the degree of its homogenisation? In the past and still today in the Third World, the city feeds off the periphery and the periphery feeds off the city, but when the periphery is no longer culturally and linguistically distinct from the city, then periphery simply becomes an extension for the city: its playground and retirement area. We now face a depressing reality that can only be defined as the suburbanisation of rural Scotland. This process can only be halted or at least slowed down by defending our indigenous cultures: Scots and Gaelic.

Official hostility towards bilingualism may be widespread but it is not based on any sound sociolinguistic data. Politicians use linguistic prejudices just as they use all other ones. David Blunket famously told immigrants that they should be talking English at home. This kind of remark is based on the mistaken belief that knowledge of another language somehow interferes with one's ability to speak English properly and to integrate. Blunkett is not alone: when speaking to a young American official at the UNHCR, who was brimming with self-confidence and certitudes, I was told that he rejected the Canadian "mosaic" solution and felt that it was not in the best interests of immigrants for them to maintain their own culture. "We prefer integration in the States. I think that *we* have to integrate *them*." I believe the opposite: the only healthy integration is one in which the immigrant community, where possible, retains its language and culture, and learns the host language and culture as an addition to its own identity. Moreover, studies show that bilingualism is a powerful educational tool, and far from eating up resources and distracting children from more important tasks, it improves children's educational performance. Recent statistics released by the Scottish Executive have shown that Chinese and Gaelic-medium schoolchildren considerably outperform other groups. Against an overall average of 172, Chinese schoolchildren scored 214, Gaelic-medium 201, Asian/Indian 191, Asian/Bangladeshi 176, Asian Pakistani 174, English 170, Black/African 169 and Black/Caribbean 124 (there appears to be no figure for indigenous, English-medium Scots, but given that they are by far the largest group, the figure cannot be far off the overall average).[14] Now it is not easy to make much sense of the figures, as they are organised along rigid racial lines that

14. Elizabeth Buie, "They are the best of the bunch", *The Times Educational Supplement Scotland*, Friday March 23, 2007.

put together people who have just arrived and those who may be second- or even third-generation Scots. Social factors obviously play an important part in educational performance. It would be more sensible in my opinion to collect data on people's linguistic background and their length of stay. A second-generation monoglot Pakistani Scot is indistinguishable from an indigenous monoglot Scot in linguistic and perhaps even in cultural terms, although social problems such as racism may divide their experience and sense of identity. However, I will try to make some broad assertions: most importantly the Gaelic-medium children (mainly, I suspect, indigenous Scots with a few English) dramatically outperform the average. The Chinese, mostly recent arrivals, are probably bilingual, while the Asian communities will be split between bilinguals and monoglot English-speakers. Indeed, the problem is not that immigrants are not integrating: it is that they are losing their languages often within a generation, and we are therefore losing a cultural resource.

There are really two arguments here: first that teaching in more than one language increases the linguistic ability of a child, and second that this also increases a child's whole educational performance. The educationalist Richard Johnstone argues,

> There is potential advantage in starting early, in that with appropriate teaching and a sufficient amount of time each week it can bring children's intuitive language acquisition capacities into play. This may help them over time in acquiring a sound system, a grammar and possibly other components of language which have something if not everything in common with a native speaker's command.[15]

---

15. Richard Johnstone, *Addressing the "Age Factor": Some Implications of Languages Policy* (Council of Europe: Strasbourg, 2002), p. 19.

Johnstone is talking not about bilingual teaching but teaching a foreign language. With various caveats, he admits that earlier is better, which happens to agree with a widely-held view based on personal experiences. Younger is better, although people can always learn languages. Above the age of seven or eight, children are more anxious about foreign language acquisition. He also claims that early language learning "fosters important underlying qualities such as a child's literacy, language awareness, and personal development (social, emotional, psychomotor and cognitive)".[16] This reference to personal development seems to me to be particularly important. Many observe that in the more extreme example of bilingual education, children appear more relaxed and less aggressive. If you accept that a child's very large brain (90% of the size of an adult brain at the age of five) is designed for the mammoth task of language acquisition, then enlarging the task is not stressing the child but providing it with an environment in which it can do what it does well.

Sadly both Conservative and Labour governments have been reducing language teaching in Britain, possibly on the spurious basis that English-speakers no longer need to learn other languages. The British Academy has recently stated,

> Language training and take-up at GCSE and beyond in secondary schools is inadequate to support the development of high-level graduate studies and academic research in the humanities and social sciences. Research in all subjects is becoming increasingly insular in outlook, because PhD students do not have language skills, or the time to acquire them.[17]

---

16. Johnstone, p. 19.
17. *British Academy submission to the Dearing Review*, "Summary", Para. 2.

As far as I am concerned, education should be about creating intellectually alive and balanced human beings who will decide as young adults what they want to do with their lives, but as we live in simple pragmatic times obsessed with the vocational, I would like to point out that two widely spoken languages amongst our immigrant communities are Chinese and Urdu, which is very closely related to Hindi. All languages are for me valuable assets, but Chinese and Hindi are the languages of the two rising world powers. Surely even the pragmatists should be able to realise that these are important resources.

I would like to make a suggestion to our educationalists and politicians. We should start to see the introduction of "foreign languages" into our society as an opportunity rather than a problem. Of course, adults who do not speak English would be well-advised to learn the language in most cases (although not all, and the idea of testing applicants for British citizenship or immigrants in general is a mistaken one). The current government's oafish approach to language issues is typified by Ruth Kelly's statement to the *Politics Show* on BBC1: "I do think translation has been used too frequently and sometimes without thought to the consequences. For example, it's quite possible for someone to come here from Pakistan or elsewhere in the world and find that materials are routinely translated into their mother tongue, and therefore not have the incentive to learn the language [sic]."[18] The idea that someone would give up learning a language simply because of the provision of a few translations is so absurd that it is hardly worthy of debate. Another language is difficult to learn in adulthood, particularly if the learner is a monoglot. I don't know if Ruth Kelly speaks more than one

---

18. Will Woodward, "Translation can discourage integration, says Kelly", *The Guardian*, 11/06/07.

language, but she certainly benefits massively from the provision by foreign governments of material in her own language. Even those immigrants who have learnt very good English as adults would probably prefer to read important documents in their native tongue, as any misunderstanding might have damaging consequences (Kelly was talking about information provided by councils and the NHS, which probably use a very different register of English from the one the immigrant has learnt through living in Britain). If she is genuinely concerned about this question, she should be encouraging the government to invest more in free English-language courses for immigrants (but all we hear of is cuts). Children, however, will unfailingly learn English, usually with the local accent. If they are isolated, then the family will inevitably be thrown back on their own resources when it comes to keeping their own language alive in the next generation. If numbers are discrete, then government could provide resources for a school in that language to provide tuition for a few hours a week over an area wide enough to bring in sufficient children. If there is a concentration of a particular language group, the government could provide resources for bilingual schools in English and the other language.

This is a truly revolutionary proposal and I can sense the horror it will arouse not only amongst the bigoted but also amongst right-minded liberals like the man from the UNHCR. Calm reflection will show that the idea has many merits: it should be immediately made clear that to work such schemes would have to be open to all children in the area and would therefore constitute a resource for both the immigrant and the indigenous families. I visited a bilingual school in Slavia on the Italian side of the border between Italy and Slovenia. The school applied a system of complete equality between the languages: one week the morning lessons would be in Italian and the afternoon ones in Slovenian, and the following week it would be the other way round. All subjects were taught in both languages with the exception of those that were closely related to one of the languages: so Italian literature and Italian history were taught in Italian and Slovenian literature and Slovenian history in Slovenian. The other subjects were not separated out, so a biology class in Italian would pick up where the last one in Slovenian left off. The school was attended by children from both Slovenian and Italian-speaking families, and both languages appeared to be spoken in the playground. In other words, the school was perfectly bilingual and it turned out perfectly bilingual children. Most importantly it was a means for drawing the two communities closer together; it was integration on the basis of complete equality.

There is a note of caution to this story. There are two other Slovenian-speaking areas in Italy (Trieste/Trst and Gorizia/ Gorica), and there relations between the two communities are not particularly good. They are areas where Slovenian peasants were introduced following widespread destruction and depopulation left by a Turkish army during the sixteenth century. Slavia, on the other hand, has been Slovenian-speaking since the eighth century and, after the wars between the Frankish and the Byzantine empires, it found itself just on the western side of a new border between eastern and western Europe. During the period of the Venetian Republic this translated into a privileged role in defending the passes against attack from the east. The Republic was not known for its kindness to its mainland territories, but for strategic reasons it gave Slavia the right to elect two consuls to be sent to Venice and insisted on peasant ownership of the land rather than aristocratic estates. As a result of these ancient liberties, the people of Slavia developed a firmly entrenched identity as Slovenian speakers belonging to a western European and "Italian"-speaking environment. It seems quite possible then that a bilingual school of the type I have just described is only workable in areas where the two communities in question have reasonably good relations.

Social problems should never be underestimated, and politicians rarely lead from the front. However, the educational advantages of having bilingual schools in say English and Punjabi or English and Polish are undoubted. Above all there would be enormous educational advantages, and the social advantages would not be negligible. It would be particularly advantageous to children of monoglot English-speakers, as some parents are finding out in the case of Gaelic. In a sense, it does not matter what the other language is, as all languages can provide the extra stimulus and an opening to a different world.

Such ideas would of course face a great deal of hostility and indeed incredulity. One of the strangest things about dominant languages is their misplaced sense of insecurity. In spite of the unprecedented linguistic hegemony of American English, many Americans worry about the future of their language. While English is beamed into literally millions of non-English speaking households around the globe (particularly in small countries where the costs of dubbing are prohibitive and it is more usual to use subtitles), troubled Americans have formed an organisation called English First, although it should really be called English Only. Ten years ago their rather bizarre website was prey to a hysterical dislike of Clinton and his fiendish multilingual plot, which seemed to have been triggered by a few bilingual signs in hospitals and the fact that information on welfare rights had on occasion been provided multilingually. Today they are only marginally less frenzied and are concerned about the effects of Clinton's Executive Order 13166. I cannot say that I really know what this Order specifically intends to do as it is written in a language that must be a close relation to New-Labour-Speak. Stakeholders are to be consulted – I can tell you that – but mainly I think that several government agencies will be talking to each other and exchanging reports. I don t think that the members of English First should be losing too much sleep over this. As for Mel Martinez, their new primary hate object, he seems to be guilty of having uttered a few Spanish words from the Senate floor.[19] In fact Spanish is the source of all their nightmares, but if they bothered to look at the statistics, they would find that Spanish is going the same way as all other immigrant languages, namely into oblivion. For me, this is very sad. A growing Spanish-English bilingual community could have constituted a cultural bridge between the two Americas, and might have helped North America out of its monolingual mindset.

Spanish is no better in Latin America. More indigenous American languages have survived in the South, but this must be at least partly due to the fact that Central and South America were more populous and their political organisations more developed when the Europeans arrived. However, Latin America does contain one shining example that gives encouragement to sociolinguists and language campaigners around the world. It is the case of Paraguay and its indigenous language Guaraní. Since 1992, Guaraní has been an official language alongside Spanish (one of the surprisingly few cases of twin official languages), but the roots of its significant role in Paraguayan society go back into the nation's history. The European settlers adopted the language as well as passing on Spanish to the indigenous population. The situation is slightly diglossic: Spanish inhabits the formal world

---

19. He appears to have said, "El juez Gonzales es uno de nosotros, el representa todos nuestros sueños y esperanzas para nuestros hijos." Pretty banal stuff and surely understandable to anyone with even the most rudimentary knowledge of the Americas' other great lingua franca.

and Guaraní the informal one, but it would also appear that speakers have full command of both languages – courtship apparently commences in Spanish and ends in Guaraní. The result is a rate of bilingualism in excess of 90%, and a strong identity for the Paraguayan nation.

The American example shows the absurdities of linguistic paranoia, and the Paraguayan one shows the great cultural benefits of bilingualism, particularly for small nations.

One of Scotland's indigenous languages, Scots, is what the sociolinguist Joshua Fishman would define as an *ausbau* language, from the German for "remove from" or "build away from". This refers to the fact that the *ausbau* language is "genetically" similar to the dominant language, and therefore can gradually distance itself from its more powerful cousin. Other examples are Catalan in relation to Spanish, Frisian in relation to Dutch and Venetian in relation to Italian. Clearly we are talking about the relationship between state and non-state languages here, because Dutch, for instance, is not dissimilar to the North-German dialects that surround it, but Dutch is a national language and has the prestige that goes with that. Should Frisian discover the political will, it would be easier for it to regain its lost ground than it would be for a non-*ausbau* language. Spanish is a national language and for a large part of the twentieth century a brutal dictatorship did all it could to extirpate all the other languages within Spain's borders. Catalan was able to find the will to re-establish itself as the national language of Catalonia in a very short period, partly because it is an *ausbau* language and partly because its geographical position close to the principal European markets has turned it into an economic power-house. Non-*ausbau* languages, such as Gaelic and Basque, are brittle and can break. If they lose ground, it takes a long time to regain even a small part of it, because they are more difficult to learn for those speakers of the dominant language who wish to return to a language lost by their forbears. Their only advantage is that they are less open to contamination. Modern speakers of Venetian are often not speaking Venetian but are actually using Italian vocabulary that has been adapted to Venetian phonology (accent) and morphology. This may also be the case with Scots, but it would be a reasonably easy task for an education system to regenerate the lost vocabulary as speakers have retained the phonology, grammar and perhaps most importantly the spirit of the original language.

This is not to say that languages like Scots and Catalan lack distinctiveness. I have heard Edwin Morgan, the distinguished poet and translator, read his translation of a Latin bucolic *carmen* (or lyric poem) into Scots. He explained that he chose Scots rather than English because he wanted to subvert the original, and ridicule its idealised view of country life. Scots, it seems, is very good at irreverence. Without any personal knowledge of the language, I sense that its shares the plain-speaking of English but is devoid of the pomposity occasionally displayed by my native tongue. Scots is itself, which means that it is a more Anglo-Saxon language than English. It is not the child of English, but the slightly crabbit parent or perhaps Northumbrian uncle who speaks with a Gaelic accent (to use the proper linguistic term, Scots has a Gaelic substratum). English, on the other hand, is the spoilt child who went off and got the fancy foreign words and diction. There is no reason why Scots could not be resurrected – not to replace English but to live alongside it, so that each can enrich the other. Today the only place this regeneration could be started is in the schools. Scots-medium education is only prevented by a lack of imagination amongst our political class.

How can we retain at least part of the variety of our languages? Minority or non-state languages fall into two categories, which I will call the "weak" and the "strong" for the want of a better term. I have not used "endangered", as all these languages are endangered to some extent; indeed, such is the pace of globalisation that even some state languages are endangered in the long term. Both Scots and Gaelic fall into the "weak" category, and for that reason bilingual schools are not good enough. English is so pervasive that the children will pick it up almost in the air; they need an initial concentration on the weak language in the early years at school, as is provided by Gaelic-medium and could be provided by Scots-medium. "Strong" languages are strong in a relative sense, and are often minority languages that are state-languages elsewhere. This gives them a foreign sponsor as well as a continuous flow of cultural products. Languages can move from one category to another: Welsh has arguably shifted from the weak to the strong category, while Catalan has undoubtedly shifted from the strong to the state category and by so doing it has shifted Catalan in the Alghero region of Sardinia from the weak to the strong category. There can be no doubt about it: weak languages will die very quickly where they are not assisted by central government. We would not let our great cathedrals and other national monuments crash to the ground, so why do so many look on with indifference at the destruction of something fashioned by endless generations of people – by an act of collective creativity across millennia? In reality, the sums of money are not enormous, in spite of the hysterical rants of those who have a voice in our societies. Speakers of minority languages are also taxpayers, and very probably they and their ancestors have been paying for their own culture to be destroyed for many centuries. Each language has its own peculiar problems: some lack a clearly defined heartland and are reduced to various pockets scattered over a large area (Irish), others have an ageing demography (Breton and Sardinian), others have lost their will to survive (Sami) and yet others face not only neglect but also state repression (Kurdish). Some languages suffer from a mixture of these complaints, although not to the same degree. To some extent, Scottish Gaelic suffers from the first three, but the indicators are not extreme, so the language could be saved if its speakers and our politicians really wanted it.

Fishman has stated, "In language as in business, nothing succeeds like success."[20] Actually this is probably true of any human activity, but it is particularly true of language. Given that Fishman has used business as his analogy, I will stick with it: languages are like assets in a free market; their worth reflects the value attributed to them by both speakers and non-speakers. The fact that everyone wants to buy into English only increases the number of people who want to buy into it. In a global market, this can have the same destructive effects on the linguistic environment that unregulated trading in raw materials can have on the ecological environment. But the state can and should intervene and regulate. Of course, it always has in the past, but only in order to strengthen the powerful languages even more than before. Today, some small steps to reverse this process have been taken, but usually on the basis of too little, too late. Successes in small languages are not dramatic affairs but they do start to change the perception or the stock of a language, and increase the chances of further successes. Once confidence has been restored to some degree, speakers can see a future for the language and work to rebuild it or to stop further decay.

---

20. Joshua Fishman, "Maintaining Languages: What Works and What Doesn't Work", in Gina Cantoni, *Stabilizing Indigenous Languages* (Flagstaff: Northen Arizona University, 1996).

Our relationship with the languages we speak is very personal. Siblings from the same family with exactly the same upbringing and perhaps little age difference can have very different linguistic personalities. One may acquire a local language or dialect and the other fail to. One may reject the linguistic stimuli triggered by an itinerant family life and the other may be irresistibly drawn to them. Where a language or dialect lacks prestige, there will always be some who wish to distance themselves from their linguistic roots. This is the slow attrition that almost every minority language suffers; this is the friend of homogenisation. However, there is nothing natural about it; it reflects the constant allure of power, particularly when there is a degree of social mobility, however small.

For an excellent example of this process, we can return to the recent history of Catalan. During the period of outright repression under the Francoist regime, speaking Catalan was an act of rebellion and certainly not the route to good jobs and social status. It clung on because there was sufficient national identity and attachment to the language, but inevitably it would have died if there hadn't been a change in regime. In the new autonomous Catalan state, the immigrants from Spanish-speaking areas send their children to Catalan-medium schools because they see this as the way to improve their children's chances in life, and as Catalan is an *ausbau* language with a long-established literary tradition, regeneration has proved relatively simple. The dominance of Spanish and the survival of Catalan have nothing to do with inherent qualities in either of these languages, and it is worth restating that there is no natural environment for language (or not since our hunter-gatherer ancestors) and it is all a matter of politics and power.

It is worth restating this, as people will forever say, "Is there a place for Gaelic / Navajo / Warlpiri in the modern world? Do they have the right vocabulary? What is their word for television?" (Warlpiri is an Aboriginal or Koori language, and interestingly Koori languages do not appear to have spread by military campaign but instead very gradually in what may well have been a kind of natural linguistic environment). These languages will find a place in the modern world, if their speakers achieve sufficient political clout, as in the case of Catalan, Quebecois French and Modern Hebrew. This last example is unique and involved the resurrection of a dead language – a language that was purely liturgical even at the time of Christ, as by that stage Jews were speaking Aramaic. That must be a harder task than "modernising" a language that is still being spoken, and yet it has been achieved. This is an extremely important point, because a large part of the social mind is not recorded (tangible) but carried within the individual minds of a language community. If a language, even one with a large literature like Hebrew, dies or almost dies and can then be resurrected, this is evidence that the social mind is capable of healing itself, although it will of course never return to what it was before.

I should make clear before proceeding any further that personal choices of language certainly do not only reflect power, although this is the case once you start to look at populations. As individuals we are capable of anything, and few can have had such a curious linguistic history as that great eccentric intellectual Elias Canetti. He was born a Bulgarian Sephardic Jew. Like many European Jews his family was both cosmopolitan and patriarchally static (a rather clumsy term to describe a complex reality). The male line was static, but his mother and paternal grandmother came from elsewhere, and indeed the latter came from Turkey, which provoked in Canetti a strange kind of Eurocentric intolerance untypical of the man. As a small child, he therefore spoke Ladino (a language very closely related to Spanish and spoken by the Sephardic community) and Bulgarian, which he lost, as it was not considered any more than a necessity for communicating with servants and tradesmen. His father wished to break free of an oppressive patriarchal situation and chose to move to Manchester, where Canetti learned English. Only when he was eight did he move to Vienna and then Zurich, where he learned German, a language in which he wrote and to which he remained utterly loyal throughout the rest of his life, even though much of it was spent in England and he took out British citizenship. The instructive part of this story is the reason for his great attachment to German, at least according to the autobiography of his childhood, *The Tongue Set Free*. His parents, neither of whom were native German-speakers, always spoke to each other in German, because they had met in Vienna and were great admirers of Viennese culture. He felt excluded from his parents' personal language and always wished to know it. German appears to have become associated with cosmopolitanism and cultural openness, in spite of the events that were shaking the German-speaking world. But then Canetti did not think in the present and no one could accuse him of what I call chronological provincialism. You can fall in love with a language just as you can fall in love with a person, because a language has a personality and it also has emotional associations.

We worry today about our lack of physical exercise. We no longer walk, and most of us are engaged in some kind of sedentary occupation. My father's contempt for those who are "chained to a desk" would now amount to a condemnation of most people working in the West. To compensate for this inactivity, we rush off to the gym and develop absurd amounts of quite useless muscle (I do not speak personally here). But how conscious are we of our mental inactivity and our neglect of that strange grey oily sponge we call a brain? Languages are not just a means to become linguists, but exercise machines for becoming better doctors, lawyers, journalists, etc. Languages are dropped from school curricula as unnecessary things that take away time from "practical" subjects, but nothing is more practical than developing the language skills of our children in order that they can do other things better.

In this context, what Marx called "national refuse" has become a resource for creating complex mixes of language built around the lingua francas I will discuss in Chapter Seven.[21] A healthily multilingual society is more aware of what it is and how it relates to the rest of the world. If we allow our cultures to be driven solely by the free market and to become the dumping ground for low-grade cultural products mainly, but not only, from the United States, then we will find ourselves in a dysfunctional, homogenised and depressingly impoverished world. Cultural products in national states can be defended by a sensible mix of cultural protectionism and reciprocity. Cultural products in small languages ("lesser-used languages" to use the correct E.U. terminology) will have to be subsidised. Cultural products are not like consumer goods; they affect the psyche of a society and a dearth of them will interfere with the generational transference of the social mind. This is not a call for cultural autarchy, and the importation of some cultural products from a wider range of sources is an excellent idea. It is however a plea for a system that is not simply laissez-faire, but takes responsibility for the important outcomes of cultural

---

21. Marx, who I greatly respect as a thinker and writer, has been proved right on some important points. That a writer like him should be so contemptuous of such peoples, amongst whom he included fairly large groups like the Czechs, says a great deal about the power of the great-nation superiority complex of the nineteenth century, which is not entirely a thing of the past. For an excellent appraisal of Marx, see Francis Wheen, *Karl Marx* (London: Fourth Estate, 1999).

policies without interfering with individual freedoms. Not an easy task, but one that deserves to be thought about in greater depth.

Chapter Six

Register

A meeting of international importance took place in the seaside town of Inverness on Cape Breton Island. Its aim was to restore Gaelic to its former glory, both in its native land and in the various communities flung like so many pebbles by the random forces of empire. No less. The venue, being the Prince Charles Hotel which had been decaying for as long as anyone could remember, was hardly deserving of so distinguished a purpose. Nevertheless the Reverend Angus Murdo MacLeod of the Permanently Presbyterian Church of Scotland was there to add his divine support to the cause.

It has been noted that if the notions of his own particularly strict faith were indeed true, then Gaelic would at least be the majority language in heaven. And given that his mother was called Angusina and his maternal grandfather Angus too, it is quite possible that Angus is the majority Christian name in heaven. Of course, it may also be that there are different heavens for each religion, which would be a more equitable way of rewarding all that energy expended on blind faith. In that case, the heaven for the Permanently Presbyterian Church might be surrounded on all sides by large faiths from which it is separated by high walls. On one side there might be the Catholic Church and on another the Sunnis, while if it were at the centre of a cross connecting four religions, it might also buttress against the Orthodox Churches and the Shias. Thus it would resemble a corner-shop surrounded by four supermarkets, or a peasant's freehold by four immense estates or latifundia belonging to Arab businessmen and American pop stars. And in spite of its marked absence of ecumenical tolerance, *its comfortable certainties and its passion for judging others, the Permanently Presbyterian Church is not without a certain quixotic grandeur; it returns the vacuous stare of modernity with its own one of proud and unflinching inflexibility.*

The Reverend MacLeod from Stornoway in the old country climbed up to the platform to make his speech. He is a small man with an enormous and vaguely threatening presence. He also dresses entirely in black and wears an old-fashioned homburg, and can be seen darting about town with the look of a someone whose divine business is not only demanding but infinitely more important than that of the two bank managers, the Lord Lieutenant, the Vice-Convenor, the MP, the MSP, and the Director of Education – all put together. The Reverend MacLeod is a man charged with a mission, and the survival of Gaelic is only a small part of the task that lies ahead of him. Hence he was a little more relaxed than his usual self, which is still a great deal more severe than most of us can ever be, and that includes his brother Calum who owns a croft in Ness, drinks the odd bottle of whisky, sleeps with the publican's wife and writes scurrilous poetry in the old tongue lampooning the worthies of Lewis and raising the poor reverend's blood pressure.

The Reverend MacLeod is not without a sense of humour, but he keeps it well harnessed. So the assorted language campaigners who made up his audience, most of whom were secular intellectuals who in the previous two or three decades had only darkened the door of their church for the unpleasant task of burying their nearest and dearest, were uncertain as to whether the title of his speech wasn't some kind of a joke: "The future of the feminine dative in the twenty-first century". The clergyman was of course doing what all clergymen do: he was starting with the specific and enlarging it to cosmic dimensions. He finished his speech, during which his listeners had the uncomfortable feeling that the decline in the Gaelic language was in fact being considered a direct result of low church attendance, with the following memorable words:

"I tell you now that there will always be the final slenderisation of the feminine dative in our Gaelic language, or it will be our Gaelic language no longer." The audience applauded with unexpected enthusiasm, perhaps in part because everyone wanted time to work out exactly what the final slenderisation of the feminine dative might sound like. They certainly did not want to give the impression that they were soft on the question of the decline in grammatical correctness.

As the exhausted conference-goers flocked out onto the street for their mid-morning tea break, they passed Mrs. MacPherson, the last Gaelic-speaker in Inverness, that is in this Canadian Inverness. It was not that Mrs. MacPherson had been childless: she had two daughters and a strapping great son who had moved to the United States, where he had obtained celebrity status for his prowess in ice-hockey and egg-eating competitions, but somehow she had failed to hand them down the language which was so much part of her being. She alone understood these curious, earnest strangers who congregated in huddles of disenchanted men and a few women outside the Prince Charles Hotel to speak ill of those other conspiratorial huddles, or so it appeared to Mrs. MacPherson. Of course, she could not understand absolutely everything they said, because they used a lot of fancy words. For instance, she didn't have words for "feminine gender", "dative" or "slenderisation", but what neither she nor the language campaigners she overheard knew was that she was someone who quite instinctively always slenderised her feminine dative, even when she was speaking to the cat, but then the cat was now the only living creature with whom she regularly conversed in Gaelic.

Not only is our diversity of languages around the world under threat, but also the languages within our languages which we call registers – the different ways we express ourselves in different social contexts. It would not be too much of an exaggeration to say that we now speak in the same way to our parents, our children, our friends, our enemies, our employers, our employees, our spouses and our lovers. Gone are the days in which Italo Svevo's character Zeno Cosini (*The Confessions of Zeno*) agonised over whether he should propose an affair with his would-be lover in Italian or in dialect. It goes without saying that the proposal of marriage, which occurred in another chapter, had to be in the standard language. When it comes to language, the human mind can be very subtle and it learns a nuanced sensitivity to what is appropriate in a given social situation. In the sixties, we teenagers of the time used to laugh at the way our mothers shifted into "posh" language on the phone. It was seen as affected and reflecting an acceptance of the class structure. It may be time to reconsider that interpretation: perhaps their change of register simply denoted the greater linguistic sophistication of women compared with men. Women, of course, have been accused of senseless garrulousness since time began, but garrulousness is no waste of time – it is the path to a command of language and of different types of language. But things have changed: the language of men and the language of women are now much less dissimilar than they were twenty years ago. That too is part of the flattening out of the linguistic universe.

The problem for an egalitarian is that much of the diversity within language was based on social hierarchy. Sociolinguists come up with eccentric societies that have different "languages" for men and women,[1] or for different classes. An example of the former is an extinct Arawak language and an

---

1. Charles de Rochefort's *Histoire naturelle et morale des Îles Antilles* (2nd edition, Rotterdam, 1665) tells the story of such societies in the Antilles. Grammar did not change, but about one in ten of the words he recorded changed between the sexes. This is not another language, but another register. See Otto Jespersen, *Language: Its Nature, ...*, pp. 237-8. The language difference clearly reflected the degree of social division between the sexes, as Rochefort tells us that "the women do not eat till their husbands have finished their meal" (*Histoire ...*, p. 497).

example of latter is Javanese which has five clearly distinct status styles. There is an informal style or "language" (*ngoko*), a intermediate one (*madya*), a deferential one (*krama*), a highly deferential one (*karma inggil*) and one for the royal court (*basa kedaton*). These are merely highly structured and formalised examples of something that exists in all societies. Where there were any divisions in societies, there were also linguistic distinctions, which in some cases were highly formalised and therefore called "languages". These distinctions, but not necessarily the divisions that underlie them, are disappearing, because of a process of compression mainly driven by the mass media and the technologies that make them possible.

Register concerns our ability to shift the manner in which we speak to conform to our situation: this may refer to our social situation or it may refer to the familiarity of a situation. If a situation is familiar to both speaker and listener, the speaker can use a kind of shorthand that does not require full sentences, because a great deal is understood by both parties. Let us take an extreme example. The expression "over there!" does not constitute a full grammatical sentence in English, but in many cases it would be more than adequate for its purpose, and anything more would be redundant. It could mean "Go over there!", "He is over there" (two people are looking for a man and one has just seen where he is), "Throw it over there", "Look over there", and so on. In context, there would be no doubt about the meaning and this is not an example of inarticulate speech.

Tom Shachtman makes this point in *The Inarticulate Society*, a study of the problem which provides some interesting data on the commodification of cultural products in the United States. His arguments are however trapped within the American monolingual mindset, and his rather dismissive views on non-literate societies (based on the work of Luriya, a Russian sociolinguist) are not convincing in my opinion. But Shachtman is surely right when he argues that American schools have abandoned the teaching of "articulate behaviour", and we would have to extend his comment to our own British schools. He starts his second chapter with the fairly banal example of a Puerto Rican woman living in New York who intentionally loses her accent in the company of the majority community and reverts to it when in her own community. We are talking here about two varieties of English, and the shift between them. Nothing could be more normal. Unsurprisingly for an American of his time, he rejects the Sapir-Whorf hypothesis that languages affect the way we think, and therefore believes that there is no reason why we should speak differently. I agree with his argument that all children should be taught in Standard English, but I arrive at it by a very different route. Particularly interesting are his comments on Labov's championing of BEV (Black English Vernacular). Labov pointed out quite rightly that BEV is just as developed in terms of capacity for conceptual learning and has the same logic as English. But this is a truism. Labov's conclusion that BEV speakers should be taught Standard English only when they were in their teens is quite monstrous, and is rightly criticised by Shachtman, particularly as some urban districts actually implemented these recommendations, thus cutting the children off from the books and learning they, like everyone else, needed. Children, as I have made quite clear, are capable of learning different languages and different registers. Standard English does not have a linguistic or conceptual advantage, but it does have many other considerable advantages that go beyond the petty one of social prestige. It gives the speaker access to a massive speech community and even more importantly to literature and learning. It is quite natural for BEV-speakers to desire recognition for their own language, and there are two clear solutions. They can either continue to speak their dialect and learn Standard English at school, which is a situation shared by most people to some extent, or they can formalise their dialect and turn it into a language. They can invent an orthography, carry out lexicographical studies, commence a loose standardisation and start writing. In that case, they would then be well-advised to introduce bilingual education: part of their lessons in Standard English and part of their lessons in BEV. It is to be hoped that someone would also invent a better name for the language than BEV or Black English Vernacular (a name that has American anthropologist stamped all over it).

In countries that have more complex linguistic realities (most of the world), this kind of thinking would appear absurd, but in Britain it is depressingly familiar. When Italy was unified in 1861, between 2.5 and 5% of the population spoke Italian (according to the estimate you wish to believe). The "dialects" are still spoken in large parts of Italy, and typically an Italian dialect-speaker will have three basic levels of expression. First there is the dialect, which is generally another Neo-Latin language with or without a literature, and the dialect itself will be divided into different registers. Then there is the intermediate language, which Italians call a "Regional Italian". This is roughly equivalent to our "accent", which is phonologically diverse but not grammatically and lexically diverse, but does often involve small changes such as particular idioms and a few words, which may actually be familiar to people from other regions. Occasionally there are more significant changes such as the elision of the final vowel on nouns. Then, of course, there is standard Italian, which will include registers inherent to it, as well as the Regional Italian, effectively an extra register. Italians are much more exacting about the standard language than English-speakers. I can remember an outraged Tuscan shouting at the television when the then prime minister, a Neapolitan, was speaking. "He can't even speak Italian," my friend cried, but whatever his other faults, the poor man had only said *possibbile* instead of *possibile*. This would be the equivalent of condemning a politician from Yorkshire for pronouncing "but" like "put", and demonstrates the much higher sensitivity to register in some other cultures (in this case, I think excessive). Paradoxically, linguistic diversity in a country sometimes creates a more rigid concept of the standard language, which in reality is spoken by no one. The Tuscan friend thought nothing of his elided "c",[2] typical of the Tuscan accent, although in a formal situation like a television interview, he would probably have suppressed it.

Before the invention of writing, register was possibly limited to the distinctions between the formal poetic and the everyday, or to put it another way, between oral literature and oral speech. Writing brings about an enormous change, in part because it creates a new perception of language, but principally because it causes an increasing distinction between the written language and the spoken one. The reason for this is simple: before the invention of printing, literate societies were still predominately oral and the pace of language change was quite dramatic compared with recent centuries; hence every generation brought a greater distance between the spoken language and the founding texts of early literacy. Moreover, the earlier linguistic forms were protected by writing and became increasingly prestigious and were therefore emulated by the elite, creating a new highly artificial, pseudo-archaic language.

Some elements of the Neo-Latin languages were evident

---

2. In Tuscan, the "c" is not really elided (although Italians perceive it as such); it is actually transformed into a spirant (like our "h") when it is a single consonant between two vowels.

even during late antiquity (for instance, proscriptive grammars of the time would say, "Do not combine two prepositions' as with *ab ante*, which in Italian becomes *avanti* or even *davanti*, a combination of not two, but three prepositions). And the literate continued to read and write in Latin while it died as a widely spoken language and other spoken languages were born. In the fourteenth century, humanism started to resurrect "classical" Latin in place of supposedly "corrupt" medieval Latin, and by the time of the High Renaissance, some humanists were probably more Ciceronian than Cicero. Before printing, the relationship between the spoken language and the written one was complex, in part because of the mystery surrounding the latter. Secular and religious authorities could use that mystery to enhance their power; hence the hostility of the Catholic Church to the translation of the Bible into the vernacular. It was not the case that Latin and the various Neo-Latin vernaculars were totally divided; each affected the other and served to create a series of registers. When the educated spoke a vernacular, they allowed themselves to be influenced by Latin syntax and vocabulary, and this would in turn generate gradations of Latinate influence descending down the social classes, but within each social class, people would have been shifting their language according to social context. Medieval Latin had been "corrupted" by the vernaculars and the erudite set about rescuing the language from the "barbarisms" accumulated over centuries. This created a spectrum in late-medieval Latin between Medieval Latin and Classical Latin. Just when the classicists had achieved their victory, the printing press began to undermine Latin irredeemably. Printing reversed the process started by writing and gradually led the written word back towards the demotic.

The degree of register must vary from one language to another, and is in any case only one factor when assessing the linguistic complexity of a society. Two other factors that are of great importance are geographical diversity and chronological diversity (still within the same language). To some extent, register is a crystallisation of these two factors within a social context: the most prestigious varieties of language will originate from a certain period and a certain place, but will be transformed by their adoption as the upper registers. Registers serve various purposes, not least that of providing satirists with something to subvert. Excessive degrees of register are probably the sign of a hidebound and hierarchical society.

However, we should stop seeing language or ideal language as a monolithic block. Languages should have different registers, and by negotiating our way through them, we create our own personalities. I started this chapter with the example of the slenderisation of the feminine dative, and I will not burden the reader with exactly what that is. It is sufficient for our purposes here to know that it is rapidly disappearing from spoken and, very probably, written Gaelic. Some might consider its retention an act of pointless pedantry, and others might consider its disappearance an act of linguistic indolence. Most sensible people would not care too much either way, but if they are speakers, they are still left with the decision as to whether they should slenderise or not. This is a very personal decision, which is affected by aesthetic, social and linguistic considerations. Sophisticated Gaelic-speakers may decide that they will use both forms, and in English and indeed all other languages, we make such decisions all the time, although mainly in an unconscious manner. In some cases, the use of the subjunctive in English sounds stuffy, and in others it can be incisive. Register is ultimately a tool that provides our languages with extra layers of subtlety; we should not let it die.

Chapter Seven

The need for a lingua franca and its inherent dangers

I am a man. I am a man and I must defend my country. My father told me this before we left home. "You can come, but your brother is too small". My brother cried in anger. But I am a man. The rifle is heavy in my hands, and my father occasionally adjusts its position, while telling me to be a man. He pats me on the back. Be strong! The owner of the flat we are in makes us tea, and the neighbours – a doctor and his nervous wife – beg us to leave. "You'll get us all killed," she screams. She weeps. "It's no good," she tells her husband. He shakes his head. "It will make no difference," he says, "they have tanks and planes. You cannot stop them." "It is our country," my father cries, exasperated by a people who do not want to be free. They leave. And we wait. Then the noise starts. A mixture of noise. Gunfire, grenades, shouting, screams. A solitary plume of smoke rises behind the houses on the other side of the street. But the noise doesn't seem to get closer. Will they never come? Finally a tank appears and moves like a giant toy. Its clockwork motion is part of a bigger machine that is going to eat us up. We all fire. I only shoot once, as the rifle leaps in the air and almost breaks my shoulder.

But now things are moving fast. There are boots on the stairs and automatic fire. Father shifts, and touches me on the shoulder, as if to check that I am still there, even though I am right next to him and breathlessly whimpering with fear. They break into the flat and fire their guns at the same time. Everyone falls to the ground except myself. My father's cousin moves. He is bleeding badly and a soldier shoots him in the head in the same way that my mother cuts a chicken's neck. Perhaps more callously. Another man stands before me, and my stomach and legs turn to water. I can hardly stand. And in as much as I can think, I think that I too am about to die. The man is very big and broad, and has a bloated red face. He smiles. His breath is laboured and smells terribly. These devils are going to kill me and I will never see my mother and my brother again. He shouts at me in a strange language and tears the Lee Enfield from my hand. I forgot that I still had it. He shouts again and slaps me round the face. I do not understand what he is saying, and his language stinks as much as his breath. Now he is even angrier, and he is screaming at me, as though I were a fool. Then I notice that he is occasionally pointing to the door, and I begin to understand. He wants me to go. He is telling me to go somewhere – home probably. My legs that were jelly now find a new strength, and as the idea quickly crystallises in my head, my reflexes return. Suddenly I am at the door and rushing down the stairs. The doctor lies dead on the landing and his wife further down. I leap over them and almost slip on the blood. Another soldier comes out onto the landing to shout some more of that filthy language down the stairwell. I run faster, discovering new sources of energy and without a thought for my dead father. Just life. I want life. I run for several blocks without looking back, and the firing continues all around. In a quiet street, I suddenly find that all my strength goes. I am alone and I start to shake.

A door opens and a woman appears. "Auntie, let me in. The British are here and want the canal. They are killing everyone. Let me in please." "Of course, little one. I saw you running and have opened the door for you." I like being called "little one". "Little one" fills me with reassurance and at the same time makes

me want to cry. "Auntie, what kind of a language is British?"
She smiles as she bolts the door. "Where do they speak British,
auntie?" She sits me down on a chair and says she will get me
something to drink. "Why do they go around the world as though
it were theirs, and why do they speak British as though everyone
should understand them."1

Language divides us. Anyone who has ever travelled in a
country whose language they do not know, will have discovered how the most banal activities can suddenly become
very complex. This is part of the pleasure of travel, and the
traveller experiences the world in a different way. The discovery of someone who has a shared language becomes an
event, while at home it would have been an assumption.
Language should be one of the identities that most moti-
vates our actions and conflicts, after all it is one of the few
identities that is based on a clear analytical distinction, the
only other one being sex (language is provided by society
and sex by biology). Nationality is an entirely arbitrary category, religions are merely a means for collecting together
often entirely contradictory ideas (is a Sufi closer to a
Quaker than to a Wahhabi?) and generation is a fascinat-
ing distinction, but we have no logical analytical method for
assessing when one ends and another starts. Languages, too,
were once more difficult to distinguish, and dialect continua
meant that the borders of inter-comprehensibility shifted
endlessly. But in the age of standardised languages, language
is a clearly detectable identity.

The division caused by languages was the inspiration for

---

1. This story is almost entirely based on elements taken from a television pro-
gramme broadcast during the fiftieth anniversary of the Suez Crisis, including of
course that of the young boy who was slapped. Interestingly, the British soldiers
admitted that all prisoners were summarily executed and expressed degrees of
regret, while their officers denied it angrily.

Ludwik Zamenhof's attempt to create an artificial lingua franca. He came from the Russo-Polish border, all part of the Tsarist Empire, whose western regions were perhaps its greatest multilingual confusion. Polish, Russian, Byelorussian, Yiddish and Lithuanian were all spoken in the area, and his own family was Russian-speaking. He was also part of that great cosmopolitan and polyglot Jewish world that played a crucial role in European culture for one and half centuries. Indeed it invented Europe before other Europeans were aware of its possibility. His was a difficult and hard-working life, and his creation was nothing short of monumental. Its rational structure was extremely elegant: nouns ended in "o" (plural "oj"), the accusative added an "n", adjectives ended in "a", and verbs end in "as" in the present tense, "is" in the past tense and "os" in the future tense. It actually very nearly succeeded, and was ultimately one of the many victims of Nazism, which could not tolerate a language invented by a Jew for the purposes of human understanding. It is interesting that so kindly, modest and selfless a man as Zamenhof could embark on so ambitious and, some might say, megalomaniacal a project as an international language. His motivation was one of human solidarity – one of the finest emotions. Nevertheless he set himself the enormous task of inhabiting the brains of humanity. It also has to be said that it was no more than an elaborate code – too rational to be a real language.

Curiously, the language barrier is not the primary cause of conflict and misunderstanding, and this tends to undermine Zamenhof's theory. The conflicts that followed the breakup of Yugoslavia only affected speakers of Serbo-Croat, with the exception of the Kosovo one, which for a long time was put on the back-burner. The "ten-day war" in Slovenia was little more than a skirmish, and Macedonia went its own way without a shot being fired. The battle was between Catholics, Orthodox Christians and Muslims, all of whom spoke Serbo-Croat. This should not surprise us, because language, which is our principal form of communication, also allows us to consolidate our incomprehension. Fanatical Catholics, Orthodox Christians and Muslims may potentially distrust or even hate each other, but they cannot argue until they know the same language. In other words, language is the means by which we understand each other and misunderstand each other, and by which we discover our similarities and our differences.

Lingua francas can unite us, particularly when the speakers are not native speakers. Lingua francas have the bad habit of obliterating the languages that they were supposed to bridge. The original lingua franca, the Neo-Latin spoken between the crusaders and the peoples they invaded, did not do this, partly because the crusaders were militarily unsuccessful in the long term and partly because it wasn't strictly speaking a lingua franca, but more probably a pidgin with borrowings from many European and Middle-Eastern languages. Lingua francas are fully developed languages generally imposed by empire, but sometimes just by trade, as in the case of Malay in south-east Asia. It cannot however be denied that they have always fulfilled an essential role, and today that role is even more important.

It may appear that I have at times been harsh on lingua francas and on English in particular. Perhaps I was being polemical about the language in which I write, and about which it is difficult to form an objective opinion, in the same way that it is difficult to assess one's own parents. Perhaps I wanted the reader, who necessarily is an English-speaker, to think more carefully about this language, particularly as there is a great deal of smugness amongst English-speakers

– the inevitable result of the language's power. To deprive a Gaelic, Scots or Welsh child of the opportunity to learn Gaelic, Scots or Welsh would amount to an act of cultural vandalism, but equally it would be an act of senseless insularity to deprive that same child of the opportunity to learn one of the world's great lingua francas, which in these cases is likely to be English (the Welsh of Patagonia providing, I think, the only exception). The greatest problem with English is entirely unconnected to its linguistic structure and its efficacy as a human language; it is simply far too dominant. It is now the dominant or official language of over sixty of the 185 nations recognised by the United Nations. Estimates of the number of speakers of English as a second language vary widely: 350 million, according to *Vanishing Voices* and between 700 and 1,400 million in *The Cambridge Encyclopaedia of Language*, while *The Times* estimates the number of competent speakers (including native ones) to be 1,900 million.[2] Presumably it is not easy to define a speaker of English as a second language. Of one thing we can be certain: these statistics are out of date as soon as they are collected, such is the unrelenting rise of the English language, which now challenges national languages and even some of the other lingua francas.

English came to dominate the popular music scene around much of the world in the late sixties and early seventies, but what was considered a passing fad at the time has turned into a permanent reality. Given the undoubted cultural influence of pop music, this is a disturbing development. Even if you are not concerned about the impoverishment of linguistic heritage, is it wise to leave a decision so vital to humanity

---

2. Daniel Nettle and Suzanne Romaine, *Vanishing Voices* (Oxford: OUP, 2000), p. 31; David Crystal, *The Cambridge Encyclopaedia of Language* (Cambridge: CUP, 1987), p. 438; and Richard Morrison, *The Times*, T2, Wednesday May 29, 2002, pp. 2-3.

to the vagaries of teenage prejudices about what is cool and what is not? This cultural dominance has been more important, in my opinion, than the forces of commercial rationalisation, although I admit that the causes of this phenomenon go back decades to the emergence of the United States as the dominant economy in the West in the immediate post-war period.

In Europe, we need to halt this process before it is too late (otherwise we will end up with two superpowers that have English as their dominant language). Europe's linguistic diversity has to be defended not only against English but against any other contender for dominance. One solution might be to give lingua-franca status to the languages of the large European states which all have populations of around sixty million, with the exception of Germany which has many more. The "core languages" would therefore be English, French, German and Italian: two Neo-Latin languages and two Germanic ones. Polish should therefore be added to represent the Slavic group of languages, even though Poland's population is considerably smaller (38 million, less than Spain's 42 million). To attain a reasonable degree of universality, this system would require every child to be fluent in at least two core languages as well as their own, which may or may not be a core one. An exception could be made for speakers of minority languages, who would learn their own language, their national language and at least one core language, although these children would often be able to deal with another core language as they usually have greater linguistic skills. This is simply one model, and it could be designed in various ways and in accordance with different criteria. The important thing is that no single language should become too dominant. The defence of the core languages would also be the first line of defence for Europe's wider linguistic diversity, and thus the non-core languages should interpret such a move as a step towards guaranteeing their own survival.

Europe is struggling to create an inclusive supranational state – a kind of voluntary and democratic empire, to which states must apply for admittance. The only problem is that it is not actually democratic and its parliament has no real powers. The commission is a kind of politburo with very limited powers and a very vague remit. This means that on the language question, as with almost everything else, the European Union is quite incapable of developing a coherent policy, and so one evolves by default. It is already happening and it is simply this: English, the winner, takes all. Given that the last two hundred years of European history have been all about the assertion of national cultures, I think the population of Europe as a whole should have the opportunity to engage in an informed debate on this question.

During those last two centuries, the choice appeared to be between empire or sovereign nation, and therefore between imperial multiculturalism or nationalist homogeneity. Previous to nationalism, the peasantry had for centuries been left to develop its own rich and complex languages and cultures, because nobody "of importance" cared what they thought. They exercised no political power, and any attempts at revolt were doomed by lack of organisation and geographical fragmentation. That richness and complexity went largely unrecorded until the nineteenth century or, in some cases, the late-eighteenth century, the very time in which these cultures started to fade. Peoples made their own musical instruments, invented their own songs, recorded their poetry generally by oral tradition and expressed themselves through an intricate series of dances, rituals and festivals.

Internally Europe in the nationalist period was anti-imperial (and imperialist outside Europe; in fact European nationalism triggered imperial ambitions abroad). Nationalism's final victory came with the First World War, and its slow demise started at the end of the Second World War, although it took some time for this to become obvious. Nationalism compresses everything onto an idealised mythical unit: the nation. It therefore suppresses the local and breaks up Empire, or at least forces it to reform its structures (as with the creation of the Austro-Hungarian Empire after 1848). Despite the revisionist wind that is blowing through this subject, we should continue to hold onto the concept that empires are oppressive realities in whatever form they take. However, it would be dogmatic not to admit that empires, as supranational states, have some positive functions: they throw many peoples and languages together, and often mingle them; they are often more accepting of minorities and the local than nation states are; and they create lingua francas which, historically, have been much less damaging to minority languages than national languages have been (paradoxically many post-colonial societies have suffered continued encroachment by the cultures of the former colonial powers).

When it comes to empire, we need to distinguish between the mercantile empires of Western Europe and the territorial empires of Central and Eastern Europe. As the European Union is a territorial supranational state, I will say little about the mercantile ones, except to point out that they were more interested in and successful at cultural homogenisation, in spite of being primarily involved in trade and having disparate and "far-flung" possessions.

Nineteenth-century Europe contained three empires that accepted or even exploited cultural diversity: the Austro-Hungarian, the Russian and the Ottoman Empires. This does not mean that there was equality of cultures, but it certainly means that the distinctions were structured and even essential to the proper workings of the state. This was particularly true of the Ottoman Empire, which divided the peoples it ruled over into *millets*. Although the word *millet* means "nation", nation for the Ottomans was a question of religion and certainly not a question of language, and each *millet* was governed by its religious hierarchy. *Millets* had different economic roles, and thus the empire became a mosaic of different peoples living together particularly in the cities, but perhaps often leading very separate lives. This uniquely structured system is described in detail in Misha Glenny's monumental work, *The Balkans 1804-1999*, and of the empire he writes:

> From the fourteenth to the sixteenth century, the imperial army swept all before it, one of the most successful machines of military conquest in history. In its wake, the Ottoman military left not only scorched earth but a unique social and political system. This was sometimes brutal but often more equitable and predictable for its subjects than the early modern monarchies of Europe. Until its collapse in the early twentieth century, the Empire remained overwhelmingly rural in character.[3]

This static and rural nature of the Ottoman Empire made it possible for both small and large "ethnic" or linguistic groups to survive with little change to their relative size; it was also the cause of the empire's centuries-long stability and ultimately its demise. It contrasted with its First-World-War ally, the new, dynamic and nationalistic German Empire, which was industrialising fast, and at the same time attempting to

---

3. Misha Glenny, *The Balkans 1804-1999. Nationalism, War and the Great Powers* (London: Granta Books, 1999), p. 70.

extirpate all cultural differences. While Tsarist Russia was something of a hybrid, the Ottoman and Austro-Hungarian Empires, for all their undoubted and differing faults, do demonstrate that linguistic diversity can be maintained for centuries without the supranational state collapsing.

The nationalist period of the nineteenth and twentieth centuries also produced "mass society", which involved both the brutal uprooting of ancient societies and their regimentation in new ones. Paradoxically, the ensuing fragmentation and migrations increased levels of individuality, individual enterprise and individual endurance within a system that wished to obliterate the individual. Or in other words, the period referred to as "mass society" produced the most essential form of difference and individualism: a turmoil of ideas. During this period, people were motivated by the type of education Marxists called bourgeois education, but it should more correctly be defined as national education based on large standardised languages and their written forms. While this was useful for rationalising trade and the bureaucracy, it caused some profound difficulties for the modern state: it enabled the powerless to speak across greater distances, and to organise. The period of "mass society", which culminated just after the Second World War and then began to die, had many ugly aspects, but it was also a period in which great popular traditions were the main source of artistic expression (the exact period varied according to the art form). Like most things concerning "progress" and rationalisation, the larger linguistic units brought cultural advantages and disadvantages: they facilitated greater inter-comprehension between dialects, but they destroyed the variety, the intimacy and indeed the ownership of language. The so-called mass society was one in which industry required a large semi-educated workforce. As semi-education often leads to excellent education, the mass of grey-clothed workers hid a great variety of individuals with different skills and educational levels.

Today, an over-active propaganda machine (typical of an age of conformity) proclaims our democracy as though it were an ancient and inviolable right, even as democratic rights are being infringed in the name of the "War on Terror". In fact, our fragile democracy is quite young. "Universal Manhood Suffrage" (to use the Chartists' term) was finally implemented in 1918 and genuine democracy (equal suffrage rights for both men and women) had to wait until 1928. These rights were not achieved by the Conservative Party, the Banks, the IMF, the armed forces and all the other people who now justify their every action by trumpeting the word "democracy"; they were achieved by the lengthy struggles first of the labour movement and then of the suffragettes. In the former movement, the working-class intellectual played the leading role, and the working-class intellectual was typically a product of a national reality.

Today, the multi-coloured consumer mass hides very little indeed: a silent lack of expression that, like a bunch of plastic flowers, sparkles in a gaudy craving to attract attention to its emptiness. The consumer mass is not cruel, but merely disinterested. It is languid and listless. It lacks passions, or takes it passions passively sitting on the sofa with a can of beer. The consumer mass lacks the brutal fanaticism or justified outrage of the physical crowd that throughout history has made its appearance, and in the first seventy years of the twentieth century made its appearance far too often – on some occasions to express its noble solidarity but on too many others to express its ugly prejudices. The consumer mass has learned some lessons and its innate cynicism has some merits. But the consumer mass is overly fragmented and unable to express its undoubted intelligence, because it has no time to stop in spite of its unprecedented leisure, and because it is through interaction between individuals that genuine individualism is created. The consumer mass therefore cares no more about the variety of human language than it does about the whales, the rainforest or aids and malaria in Africa, although it occasionally stirs on the back of "big events". Very often people do not even care about the disappearance of their own cultures.

Today Europeans may continue to drift and decline, occasionally stirring at the ugly xenophobe's goad, or it may realise that it has a future – a great cosmopolitan future that is neither nationalist nor imperialist, but a fusion of the two. The E.U., whose greatest problems are constitutional rather than cultural, could create a functional federal state that does not lead to cultural homogenisation. It would achieve this by integrating the nations under a federal parliament with real but carefully circumscribed powers. As far as cultural politics is concerned, this means the creation of careful balances between the "core languages" which could be termed official lingua francas, the national languages and the "minority" languages. It is a matter of finding the right structures, which, I do not deny, is a very difficult task.

In "post-industrial" society, the speed of rationalisation, homogenisation and extreme fragmentation has dramatically increased. These then are the trends: less variety of languages and less variety within languages. Ultimately this means less garrulous subversion and less criticism of the powerful. To overcome this haemorrhaging of our humanity, we need not only to gabble ceaselessly, but to gabble in more than one language. The soulless utilitarians argue that some languages are more useful because they are spoken by more people. This is typical of the simplistic reasoning that now governs our lives – a reasoning based on statistics that ignores the actual ways in which we behave and, in this case, the real purposes to which we put our knowledge of language. We need a language to speak in a myriad of intricate ways to the handful of close friends, relations and colleagues that for most of us suffice for life's passage, and to communicate with a larger community of strangers and acquaintances on a less complex level. But we can do this with the same richness of expression in a language of 200 thousand as we can in a language of 200 million. Indeed, the language of 200 thousand may well have avoided some of that flattening-out process that affects many larger languages. We do not intend to speak to every speaker of that language; we simply want a language to have the critical mass required for self-sufficiency. Because of the cultural economies of scale, some might claim that only the club of very large languages is capable of achieving that critical mass. One of the principal purposes of this polemical essay is to argue against that "common-sense" belief.

On the other hand, lingua-francas are extremely useful to the traveller, and always have been, although the distances involved are now much greater. Lingua-francas do not need to be fully mastered to fulfil their function. However, a good command of them is advisable for anyone who wants to use them to their full potential: they are attractively cosmopolitan and today their literatures probably reflect the diverse cultural backgrounds of their speakers. Russian can take you through most of the northern and central parts of the Eurasian landmass, the largest in the world. Portuguese can help you understand a global linguistic archipelago that is present in every continent and shares one of these continents with Spanish. English is becoming the lingua franca of lingua francas.

The solution to the dichotomy of small and large languages is simple: speak both the language of 200 thousand and the language of 200 million. If you have the energy, learn the language of 20,000 speakers, and discover the charms of its complex intimacy. Find your own linguistic permutations; practise these different instruments regularly and delight in their different tones; and do not treat languages solely as a means to an end, but also as an end in themselves, for they generate that part of your humanity that has no place and no time.

Chapter Eight

Conclusion

There is, it's said, a soul to that,
the managed man who cleanly cuts
his actions to the manner of his time,
and laughs.
A baroque well-suited hybrid of a modern man
who smiling greets me across a guarded fullness of himself.
He laughs:
The lazy Gaels who furnished him his empire on the heights,
and more besides who fell, and did not fall but vanished
in the clearing, cleaning ethnic war they fought in peace
that stopped our tongue with the Cheviot fleece.

The greater spirit thinks those greater that it meets,
but this man's spirit spurns and scoffs:
The lazy Gaels who cut and carried in the peats,
who drove the fattened cows to fatten foreign lords.
The Gaels whose houses burnt like burning weeds,
to plant the lands with fruitless Cheviot seeds.

The door is open or the door is shut,
the heart is feeling or the mind is sprung,
the skin is hardened or the soul is stung;
but this man's heart and mind are cut
and tailored to a standard form
that laughs:
The lazy Gaels that carved a culture from a sea and land
cut by grandness, harshness, divine and ancient force,

that holds hard to the centre of the things that count;
for those who listen let stories still be heard.
This soul-less soul while tramping on the tragic stage,
sees only sands surrounding some exotic bird.
      Reflections on being told that Gaels are lazy by an urbane
                     Englishman on a beach in Tiree[1]

Walking on a beach in Tiree, I met a fellow translator – an interesting, intelligent and contradictory man of the kind that make you think but also tend to prefer boldness to prudence in their own thinking. He told me that Gaels are lazy, and I answered that this sounded a little racist and besides I was a half Gael myself. That last bit of information was totally irrelevant, and he rightly ignored it in order to expand upon his theory which, according to him, was not racist but based on sound Darwinian analysis: because there is little work in the islands, the most intelligent and enterprising leave in each generation and thus impoverish the genetic stock.[2] I confess that I still found the idea crass and a little offensive. However, his assertion did get me thinking about the strange relationship between the centre and the periphery, and this immediately pointed to the exact opposite question, one that I have never been able to answer satisfactorily. Why is it that the Gaelic-speaking areas of Scotland continued

---

1. This poem will also appear in my collection of poetry, *Presbyopia*.
2. Of course, this attitude in an even cruder form is alive and well, and inhabiting sections of the Scottish middle classes (one journalist appears to have made a career of insulting Gaels and a distinguished intellectual living in Glasgow claimed he would not have wanted one of his daughters to marry an "island boy"). In the network of prejudices and racisms that sadly affect Scotland as they do every other country, the Gaels are not the most unfortunate, but because prejudices against them don't break the rules of "politically-correct", they can be uttered in "polite society" which is generally so good at keeping its prejudices hidden. My translator acquaintance was not quite so disagreeable, but for that reason his views were also more disturbing. There is certainly no intended "anti-Englishness" in my example.

to supply doctors, lawyers and other professionals, generation after generation? The Western Isles used to produce the highest percentage of graduates in the United Kingdom, and its failure to do so now may be the result of the enormous changes in university education (the numbers have increased as has the dominance of the middle classes). The more likely reasons are a decrease in genuine bilingualism and the fact that the Western Isles are no longer a periphery in the fullest sense of the term: they are more affluent and more like any other part of the country, which is what I have already referred to as the suburbanisation of rural Scotland.

The answer to my question does not lie in some kind of reversal of my urbane friend's pseudo-Darwinian theory: the Gaels live in an inhospitable terrain that has made them stronger over the passing generations. It would be absurd to use Darwin to return to racial theories that enjoyed their greatest popularity during the interwar years.[3] When Joseph Roth wanted a nationality to represent archetypal peasants in the Austro-Hungarian Empire, he thought of the Slovenians, and in accordance with the national prejudices of the time, he made them big-fisted with gummy smiles. In the nineteenth century, Slovenians were nearly all peasants as the capital Ljubljana and some of the towns were German-speaking. Like the Gaels, they were also a society in transition: moving to the towns and organising to reassert their culture. Reading clubs were set up particularly in urban areas, which included cities like Trieste, while active

---

3. Unfortunately this is exactly what is happening, but it is still at a fairly tentative stage. Consider that there was a time when even a great intellectual and man of the left like Shaw could write such lines as "the majority of men at present in Europe have no business to be alive" and "if we desire a certain type of civilisation and culture, we must exterminate the kind of people who do not fit into it." These quotes appear in John Carey's excellent work on the subject: *The Intellectuals and the Masses. Pride and Prejudice among the Literary Intelligentsia, 1880-1939* (London: Faber and Faber, 1992), pp. 62-3.

and literate Gaels crowded into Glasgow to campaign on Highland matters. The city reproduced the cultural topography of its hinterland, and in its crowded rooms the air was free from the landowner's imperiousness. I have been to Slovenia several times, and I noticed no great preponderance of large hands; as for smiles gummy or otherwise, the Slovenians struck me as a polite, well-educated but rather serious people. Like the Gaels, they have the prickliness of a people who have been driven away from power for many generations, to the detriment of their culture but perhaps to the betterment of their souls. In the twentieth century, the paths of these two politically disinherited peoples diverged dramatically: today, the Slovenians are one of the most cultured peoples in Europe and have won the battle to maintain their language, while the Gaels may have lost theirs.

The relationship between periphery and the centre has been a universal feature of human society since the invention of agriculture and international trade. I believe that one of the reasons for the cultural richness of what might be called the transitional periphery is that it is very often bilingual. Linguistic diversity constantly renews a society, and also helps in the natural process of linguistic renewal, particularly where patterns of dominance and interdependence are complex (this can even affect very powerful languages like German, which at the time of the wall coming down was divided into two mildly different categories that reflected either Soviet or Western dominance). The luckiest individuals are those who spend their childhoods in the periphery and their adulthoods in the centre, which is where ideas can be empowered. Moreover, the periphery can be claustrophobic, while those who are born in the cosmopolitan centre are often unconsciously provincial. In the past, it was possible to establish a degree of stability in this relationship: the periphery with its high demographic growth supplied the centre with new blood, while urban society atrophied those who had lived there for too many generations. Before 1800 all states were overwhelmingly multilingual, and after that date the elusive mechanisms that kept this relationship "healthy" appear to have broken down, slowly at first and at a destructive rate in recent times (I have put the word "healthy" in inverted commas, as this relationship was always an inherently abusive one, in spite of its undoubted social usefulness).

This breakdown in the machinery of language and interaction between languages is part of the homogenisation of Western society. The West itself has become the centre and the Third World the periphery, but this new global centre-periphery relationship, while as abusive as ever if not more so, does not have the same functionality as in the past. This situation is probably not going to last but in the meantime, it is going to inflict untold damage socially and, what matters here, linguistically. The Third World is irresistibly attracted to the West, and the West needs those people, even though it inflicts terrible dangers upon their inevitable migration. Many landless or cleared peasants of the Third World, who do not make it to the West, end up in an urban limbo, as they feed into the ever-growing sprawl of slum-dwellers in what are naturally called "megacities" and "hypercities". Something vaguely similar happened for a while in nineteenth-century Europe: Naples and Palermo were examples, but nothing like on the same scale. In the end, the New World provided an escape route that is not as easily available to the inhabitants of Bombay, São Paulo or Nairobi today. That nineteenth-century emigration created great expanses of monoglot English, Spanish and Portuguese that dwarfed the original linguistic communities in Europe, which in the case of Britain and Spain existed in states that were to some extent also multilingual. Today English is rushing towards dominance of both parts of a polarised globe, and the Third World is also becoming dangerously homogenised. This is very clearly expressed in Jeremy Harding's review of Mike Davis's *Planet of Slums*:

> This constant production of numbers – and a seamless access between continents – offers us the world as a single, intelligible place defined by universal laws of accumulation and deprivation. Any sense that slum cultures and slum cities might have a specific character, beyond the common lot of misery, is tenuous. No book will give readers the impression of covering greater distances, even if they will feel by the end as though they'd been cooped up in a narrow, featureless room. Homogeneity, Davis would argue, is what late capitalism does: already a billion people live in roughly the same extraordinary way in roughly similar environments. Vast, contiguous slums are the habitat of the future for ever larger numbers, yet the future looks more and more like it did the day before yesterday.[4]

It is as though the human population no longer has the antibodies to fight off a process of homogenisation that is destroying its collective social mind while at the same recording it on an unprecedented scale. Soon all the languages will be in libraries and museums, and all the cultures fossilized on tapes and in books. But who will visit them? And of those who do, what will they be able to take away? A mere shadow of the original thing.

What beckons is a monoglot world in which an Orwellian

---

4. Jeremy Harding, "It Migrates to Them", *London Review of Books*, vol. 29, no. 5, 8 March 2007, pp. 25.

simplification of language and a kind of linguistic passivity conjoin in a vicious circle. It will be a world in which there is one story endlessly retold (or consumed); it will be the paradise book-burners always desired – one in which a single text survives and there is no longer any need to burn books because none threaten; it will be a monoculture that is not aware of its own existence because it has no "other" to which it must relate.

Human beings and indeed all nature thrive on diversity and chaos, but humans have an innate drive to order that chaos, and this brings certain benefits as that victory over chaos is only partial and never complete. Our drive to uniformity has until recently been relatively harmless because it was incapable of success. All human activity found a balance between order and chaos, but now our systems are bigger than ourselves and our power to change and to order things in new ways has become almost unlimited. Our small activities are also tainted by the sophistication of our equipment, although mercifully writing has remained relatively unaffected.

Take, for example, this book which you have nearly finished. Like all human language, it is a sequence and has to be experienced as a sequence. I have attempted to order the arguments, and I have put forward various explanatory hypotheses. But of course I did not write it as a sequence: switching between chapters, I worked as I was driven by my own erratic brain; I moved text around, I added and deleted, and finally and quite arbitrarily I said, "it is done" and sent it to the publisher, even though there is never any clear reason for stopping work on any book, other than the fact that the writer might be getting bored with it. Moreover, this book is not just the product of recent readings; it is a snapshot of how my ideas and uncertainties have developed in 2007 after fifty-four years of listening, talking, reading and, in the non-linguistic realm, observing. Next year, new conversations or readings may lead me to alter my opinion radically. Even in this effort of one individual to order his thoughts (not a great achievement, one might think), chaos is always present and undefeated (partly because reality is not a sequence and cannot be accurately represented as one). I would even argue that whatever merits this book has are in part due to its inability to overcome chaos and order ideas perfectly. If it had been a better book, which does not necessarily mean a more ordered book, it would still have failed, because perfect order is impossible – it should be desired but it is not desirable as an outcome.

Order is so beloved of humanity, because without at least an approximation to it we could not think. We think through language, which is in turn the result of apparently agreed categorisation. But even in the categorisation of an object as banal as a table, we find that no one can produce the perfect definition, although we can all come up with a very good one. In reality a raised plane with varying numbers of legs or supports can do so many things, some of which are not very table-ish. Is a desk a kind of table or something entirely separate? If it is the latter, then what is a writing-table? Obviously with more complex and possibly abstract categories, we find this elusiveness of order more of a problem. But it is not just a problem. It is also the source of our being, our daily strivings: a final victory of order would destroy the essence of humanity. Chaos should also be beloved of humanity, especially now that we are in danger of destroying it through a massive unravelling of the individual mind.

The lack of equality in the world today (for Marx's prediction of an increasing distance between the rich and the poor has proved correct on a global scale) vitalises the destructive forces of globalisation and consumerism, which will continue unchecked until the damage is so great that something has to be done – sadly something fairly draconian that may sweep away the hard-won rights of the citizen, acquired over centuries of struggle. The cultural destruction, like the ecological one, will be partly irreversible. I do not, therefore, attempt to persuade everyone to switch off their tellies and start reading, writing and chattering with maniacal zeal, as this would have as much chance of success as attempting to convince humanity to forego violence and live together in brotherly love. This is not an age for slogans and certainties (although peacefulness and garrulousness are undoubtedly virtues). This is an age for attempting to salvage as much as possible from the storm of greed, wastefulness and compulsive subservience to fashion (particularly when it comes to thinking). I can say, however, that whoever does switch off the television (or even better, throws it in the dustbin) will start to engage with idleness and chatter and perhaps the odd book. These thoroughly human activities will often be psychologically beneficial. I am certainly not advocating universal bookishness, but books as an extension of our dialogues and an enrichment of our intellectual interaction can also be helpful as long as they are not accompanied by fanaticism, as in the case of Kien, the misanthropic protagonist of Elias Canetti's *Auto da Fé*, who eschewed all human relations in order to cultivate further his almost physical sensitivity towards books and whose one relationship resulted from his mistaken interpretation of another person's relationship to books (books are dialogues in the reader's head in which readers never hear their interlocutor's answers other than through the next passage – as Sartre said, reading is an "act of generosity", but it should not become an act of compulsion). Passion for books can be for the words they contain or for the objects in themselves, or indeed for both. Books can become just another form of *collezionismo*, the obsessive acquisition of any particular category of thing. But in the case of determined readers who are careless book-owners, their collections say a lot about their character and the character of their thoughts, and as Walter Benjamin amusingly and accurately pointed out, the books they haven't read say as much as the ones they have.

An excessive obsession with books, as with any other physical object, will lead to an inability to use them in a pleasant and relaxed manner governed by enjoyment of the thing in itself – a sequence of intangible words anchored in the very tangible reality of a mass of papers stitched and glued together in a single unit. Books have a feel. They have a history both as pages bound into a whole and as a sequence of words that can be constantly reprinted. Personally I always prefer to read old books in a recent edition. Old editions become objects of value, often irrespective of the text they contain, and I therefore feel they cannot belong to me. On the other hand, old editions have their charm; they should not be loved as objects, or even excessively admired – those passions should be reserved for the text. Like Ming vases, they should perhaps be attentively cared for by museum curators, but not revered and collected.

Our problems with language are not only the result of technological change which has brought a dominance of the image; they have been exacerbated by recent moves towards the extreme market economy. The shift to a society in which the individual is responsible to himself for himself and for no one else (a process that thankfully is not entirely complete) is probably something unique in the history of mankind, even though the neo-con "philosophers" would have us believe that it most closely reflects man's natural desires. The neo-con dream is a hierarchical one, but unlike hierarchical societies of the past which were often cruelly static, their hierarchy is a fluid one based on wealth. The typical *ancien régime* was a complex network of privileges and mutual responsibilities, and whatever its undoubted injustices, the resulting stasis created a climate in which language and language diversity could flourish. The modern free-market economy, in which family, community and the state are incapable of providing security, creates the social atmosphere of a perpetual shipwreck. As the population falls into the rising waters, the strongest or perhaps simply the most ruthless push their way up the masts and rigging, not to security but to a relative security which feels better when one can see so many others failing (because a shipwreck triggers the basest elements in the human psyche). Of course, there can never be security in any human society, as the neo-cons will quickly object, and every society is as exposed as a ship in fierce weather, but when people work together and engage in dialogue, they can confront their problems more calmly and even gain pleasure from their communal efforts.

If I were to paint the scene of a sailing ship going down on the rocks, I would start with the sloping deck partly immersed in the water. Here I would depict those who fall on their knees and start to pray to their gods (who are perhaps punishing them for their sins). Amongst them are wandering those who have lost the will to act and move in a daze without hope of being saved in this world or the next. Some have fainted in fear. Then I would paint the individualists who have thrown themselves into the surging sea and vainly attempt to swim towards some protruding rock, but cannot match the strength of the waves. The only people who are interacting are those who rushed to the rigging. But their interaction is the wholly tangible one of punching, kicking and pushing – desperate, dumb physicality. No one is engaged in dialogue, because dialogue would be entirely inappropriate. Language no longer has a role and, in any case, cannot compete with the shrillness of the wind. Neo-cons, not entirely without reason, will accuse me of reasoning by analogy. I will now examine these concluding arguments a little more dispassionately, but I would like the reader to bear that image in mind.

Throughout history, most people have been unable to use language to develop their understanding of the world in which they have strangely been born into consciousness. The reason is simply that they were busy with the business of survival, and society's productivity allowed leisure only for a restricted number of its members, who were not necessarily the most suited to the task of providing for their society's intellectual needs. People had to get their religions and philosophies off the shelf. Before the intellectual rigidity of the Modern Era, these ready-made religions worked remarkably well and, to take perhaps the most important examples in the West, Christianity and Islam displayed considerable tolerance, flexibility and indeed rationalism in their early periods. Inasmuch as they were rigid, their rigidity was necessary within societies with limited intellectual resources. Indeed religion generated nearly all the opportunities for intellectual discourse, and early social movements such as the Lollards naturally encapsulated their ideas within a wider religious discourse. The Modern Era liberated the minds of ever greater sections of society, and this constituted a danger that had to be managed.

I have shown how everyday language has been affected by writing, printing and the rise of the state, and how this has led to an enormous development in the Social Mind while perhaps lessening our individual linguistic dexterity. Today, other forms of industrial and communications technology mean that leisure for all is no longer an impossible dream. The fact that these developments have actually led to a society in which people work under absurd stresses or have no work at all, does not mean that some other way of organising our society is impossible. Exactly how such a society could be organised is a complex matter beyond the capabilities of my own mind and in any case not appropriate to a book on language. However, it would have to be a more egalitarian and a more educated society than our own and one in which everyone would have the leisure necessary not only for a greater use of the simpler and more spontaneous registers of language used in everyday exchanges, but also of the complex and artificial language we use to examine who we are (the ontological) and what we should do with our lives (the deontological). For the first time in history, we all have the power to become our own philosophers and, by so doing, to pull philosophy down from its unnecessary pedestal.

Since the invention of writing, the desire for riches has been contrasted with the desire for learning. This is not just a *topos*; it is the most threadbare of clichés and, if it weren't for its underlying truth, it would be embarrassing to bring up a matter that appears to be self-serving – an attempt by writers to impose their obsessions on a wider population. And, of course, this argument for less engagement with possessions and consumption and more engagement with the word can be taken too far. Epicurus, who preached a life of frugality and self-discipline, argued that extreme asceticism became just another form of fanaticism, which learning is intended to avoid (so, unlike Diogenes and the Vicar of Stiffkey, I am not advocating life in a barrel). I would go further and argue that learning is not about reclusiveness and obsessive reading (although some might accuse me of these things, and one critic did ask, "has Mr Cameron been out recently?").[5] Learning is immeasurably assisted by the written word, which gives us access to the condensed and well-ordered thoughts of others – of others who may have been dead for several centuries – but it also requires conversation,

5. Dominic Hilton, "Wrong Headed", *The New Humanist*, Sept. 2005, p. 38.

and by conversation I mean the spontaneous and unhurried exchange of sound waves structured into the mutually agreed system we call a language – that great rambling pattern of enunciated thoughts that fade like intertwined jet streams on a clear day. At the risk of sounding sententious (the ultimate crime in our cynical times), learning also requires involvement as a citizen, because without that it becomes little more than intellectual athleticism. Talking is entirely carbon-friendly and reading is not far behind it, particularly if you get your books from the library. More generally, talking, listening, reading and writing add little to our GDP, but a great deal to our well-being. Society needs to consume less, and to talk and read itself back to psychological health and a better relationship with our environment.

I do not mean, let it be clear, that man is perfectible, nor do I believe, like Marx, that one day the state can wither away. Power will remain the principal necessary evil, and some human beings will always be driven by its corrupting force, which even in the best society the state can only partially bring under control. There will never be an end to conflict in society, but rules can be devised to keep it within certain limits. My argument here is this: the soothing effects of language and education will allow more people to gain some control over the self and its insatiable wants, thus lessening the pressures within society. This is almost an Enlightenment idea, although it would not have been expressed in exactly those terms, and it is certainly a classical one. However, I also see the merits of the counter arguments: the men of 1789 were arrogant in their belief that they could create a Year Zero and rebuild society from scratch, with little understanding of what worked as well as of what patently did not work. They were not wrong in the injustices they wished to put right, but they were foolish in believing that reason can take into account all factors concerning change, and in failing to understand that we, as a species, and therefore they, as a group of overconfident young men, were and are not very good at rationalism. This failure could be called the irrationalism of rationalism. Part of the problem is human language, which has a wonderfully ungainly structure, consists of a multitude of tongues which do everything in such different fashions, and provides us with the sheer pleasure of its inefficiency. Would we want it any other way? Language, as I have said, is a gift from the past, and we should always keep our ears attuned to its subtle wisdoms.

Index

Index